The Self-Led
Internal Family
Systems Workbook

The
SELF-LED
INTERNAL
FAMILY
SYSTEMS
WORKBOOK

Learn to Use IFS Skills to Understand and Love All Your Parts

TANIS JO ALLEN, LMSW, ACSW

Foreword by Cece Sykes, LCSW, ACSW

ZEITGEIST · NEW YORK

Content Warning

The information in this book is not a substitute for psychotherapy from a qualified mental health professional. It is intended to provide helpful and informative material on the subject matter with the understanding that neither the author nor the publisher are engaged in rendering professional services in this book. The author and publisher specifically disclaim any responsibility for any liability, loss, or risk, personal or otherwise, that is incurred as a direct or indirect consequence of the use and application of any of the contents of this book. The nature and content of this book and the exercises contained in it may stimulate psychological distress for some readers. Should this occur, it is strongly advised that the reader consult a qualified mental health professional or healthcare provider.

Published in the United States by Zeitgeist™, an imprint and division of Penguin Random House LLC, New York.
zeitgeistpublishing.com

Zeitgeist™ is a trademark of Penguin Random House LLC.
ISBN: 9780593886403
Ebook ISBN: 9780593886106

Art © by Inspiration GP/Shutterstock.com, MicroOne/Shutterstock.com, urfin/Shutterstock.com
Book design by Aimee Fleck
Author photograph © by Janice Milhem
Edited by Clara Song Lee

Printed in the United States of America
2nd Printing

For my husband, Stephen Rosoff, my true partner in all endeavors, who has taught me more than he knows about my internal family system, and inspires and delights me every day

Contents

Foreword

After Internal Family Systems (IFS) founder Richard C. Schwartz left the Chicago area over a decade ago, Tanis Jo Allen saw the vital need for her IFS community to stay connected. She organized a first-of-its-kind Midwest IFS conference, the IFS Great Lakes Retreat, which has since become indispensable for a growing network of enthusiastic IFS therapists.

Now Tanis has turned her attention and considerable talents to address another vital need in the IFS community. Most IFS books are geared toward practicing therapists. *The Self-Led Internal Family Systems Workbook* is for anyone interested in a trustworthy guidebook for self-exploration and understanding. Writing in a warm, conversational tone, Tanis invites the reader to grab a cup of tea and join her for an insightful, empowering IFS journey of understanding and self-acceptance.

Unlike more traditional, single-minded approaches, the groundbreaking psychotherapeutic IFS model views the mind as made up of distinct subpersonalities or "parts," each with its own perspectives, feelings, and roles. The model also repositions the therapist to function more as a knowledgeable guide and collaborator instead of sole authority or expert in the room. In this collaborative role, the IFS therapist empowers clients to become the expert of their own system and to value their personal inner guidance, which the model labels "Self."

Tanis shares how this unique, non-pathologizing view of the therapeutic relationship naturally promotes an inherent respect in clients taking the lead in their own process. *The Self-Led Internal Family Systems Workbook* builds on this trust in self-guidance by inspiring readers to steer their own course. Tanis offers steady guidance, gradually acclimating readers to their inner landscape and equipping them with the skills they need to create strong inner relationships between their Self and parts.

The book opens with informative explanations of the nervous system, offers simple grounding exercises to create a sanctuary when readers need a break, and adds detailed examples of Tanis conducting open, curious dialogues with her own worried, frustrated parts. It continues with effective, enlightening exercises and reflections that show readers how to connect to parts, discover their crucial roles, and create compassionate, vibrant relationships within their inner world. Supportive suggestions are scattered throughout the book to address common obstacles that may arise while doing this important work.

In a world where we often feel fragmented and overwhelmed, finding a path to inner harmony can seem elusive. It is here, in our often-tumultuous inner world, that practicing Internal Family Systems can provide profound insights and practical tools for self-healing and personal growth. Whether you are an IFS newcomer or an "old hand" looking to refresh your skills, *The Self-Led Internal Family Systems Workbook* will become a trusted guide on your journey.

Cece Sykes, LCSW, ACSW

International Senior Trainer and Consultant,
Internal Family Systems Institute
Author, *Internal Family Systems Therapy for Addictions: Trauma-Informed, Compassion-Based Interventions for Substance Use, Eating, Gambling and More* with Martha Sweezy and Richard C. Schwartz

Introduction

> *Listening is the doorway to*
> *everything that matters.*
>
> —Mark Nepo, poet and artist

At its core, the Internal Family Systems (IFS) approach to psychotherapy is about learning to turn inward and listen deeply to our inner experience with curiosity and respect. It is a journey of discovering and seeking to more fully understand the true complexity contained within each of us, an internal mosaic of many different parts, each with its own set of thoughts, feelings, and needs. IFS invites us to enter into a relationship with our own internal family of parts, uncovering both the challenges and wisdom it contains, and offering it the healing energy that is unique to each of us.

Dr. Richard C. Schwartz, the creator of the Internal Family Systems model and a family therapist by training, came upon this notion of parts by listening closely to the young adult clients he was working with at the time. As many of us do, they described their thought patterns and internal conflicts with comments like: "A *part* of me wants to be able to talk to my mom, which is hard, but there is this other *part* that wants me to just go to my room, zone out, and not worry about it." He began to wonder whether all of us might have a sort of internal family composed of these subpersonalities, or parts, which operates much like a dysfunctional external family. Over time and by listening closely, he found that these parts take on particular roles, either as exiles (vulnerable parts that hold deep pain) or as protectors (parts that protect us or distract us from the exiles), and they can become conflicted or allied with one another in potentially extreme ways.

As he continued to explore this phenomenon, he came to the realization that this sort of multiplicity is, in fact, the natural state of our psyches and that there is also present in us a Self, or core essence. This Self, he learned from his clients, is not one of the parts but is that presence within us that can facilitate healing for our internal system of parts once it is accessed. This discovery and the resulting therapeutic framework that developed around it has now become a groundbreaking worldwide movement. Not only is it profoundly compassionate and empowering, but it can also bring about transformational change.

I was introduced to IFS in the mid-1990s and began training in the model a few years later. What initially drew me to IFS was its collaborative nature. The awareness that we *all*, clients and therapists alike, have parts *and* a Self that can help bring about the very healing that we most need was intriguing to me. Realizing that I had a "co-therapist" available (the client's Self) that could become fully attuned to the client's internal experience and function as an inner healer has allowed me to be more fully present to the process as their compassionate guide and companion. This has been truly transformative not only professionally but also personally, as my IFS training has involved doing my own deep personal work. The ongoing effects of this have been life-changing for me. Committing myself to this approach has profoundly impacted my effectiveness with my clients and has also allowed me to understand, trust, and love my own inner world with immense gratitude and respect.

The intention of this book is to help you get to know and love some of the many parts within you from a place of openheartedness, curiosity, and courage, which for most people is a new perspective. It is a journey you can navigate at your own pace, as there is no right way to progress on this path given the unique nature of each of our internal systems. You will be guided by exercises and explanations that will serve as a sort of trail map, though it is not likely to be a particularly linear course; there will be many opportunities to circle back as it feels right to you.

IFS invites us to slow down, let go of the need to get somewhere, and be as fully present as we can be to our inner experience. Many of us aspire to do this, but we rarely allow ourselves the time. So it makes perfect sense if this feels unfamiliar to you. Be assured that the information in this book is presented in a way that anyone can benefit from the process, especially those who are new to IFS.

What to Expect from Self-Led IFS

Because working with the Internal Family Systems model is usually undertaken with an IFS therapist, there are some differences when you practice the model on your own. The primary one is that you will not be guided to work deeply with your most vulnerable parts, which are called exiles. These are our young and wounded parts that tend to carry a great deal of pain (and possibly the effects of trauma) from the past. They are also the ones that our protector parts work hard to keep from our daily awareness. When an exile becomes triggered, we often experience a surge of intense emotions that can feel overwhelming. When this happens, it can be extremely difficult to proceed without the help of a therapist, at least when you are just beginning an IFS practice.

Considering that it is the protectors' job to keep our exiles safely tucked away, we need to solidly establish our relationships with those parts in order to earn their trust. This is the other reason you will be mostly working with your protector parts in this book. Emotional safety is paramount in this work, so it is extremely important to recognize and validate your protectors' commitment to ensuring that your vulnerable parts remain as well protected as possible.

How to Use This Book

This book is divided into two parts. Part 1 is intended to set you up for success in your IFS journey by providing a beginner-friendly overview of the model and offering several exercises to strengthen your self-awareness and ability to stay grounded. Part 2 will lead you through the IFS process by helping to orient and familiarize you with your internal world and to support you in working with the different types of parts we all have inside. The concluding chapter covers particular challenges that may arise as you continue your practice, better equipping you to navigate some predictable twists and turns along the way.

As you work through this book, notice and listen to what feels right to *your* internal system. That may come as a knowing or intuition that particular topics may take some time to sink in, while other information may seem familiar or certain exercises might feel more natural. The bottom line here is to honor and respect the pacing that is right for *you*. Remember that the point is to begin exploring your internal landscape, and not necessarily to get to a specific destination. You may want to spend plenty of time in part 1 to fully digest the information and exercises there, maybe even taking breaks and then returning to sections or repeating exercises until you feel more clarity and confidence. There is no one way to walk this path, but there is *your* way, which will reveal itself more and more as you go. Then, when you feel ready, you can move on to part 2.

In *Big Magic*, Elizabeth Gilbert notes that "you have treasures hidden within you—extraordinary treasures . . . bringing those treasures to light takes work and faith and focus and courage . . ." So know that you already possess the courage and strength this work requires within your unique, undamaged, and loving Self. And even though this journey of Self-discovery will invariably contain both fascinating and possibly challenging realizations, we each have the inherent capacity to bring healing, acceptance, and wisdom to our internal family systems, helping to reveal to us some beautiful internal treasures.

Part One

PREPARING FOR IFS WORK

What lies behind us, and what lies before us, are tiny matters compared to what lies within us.

—Ralph Waldo Emerson, poet and philosopher

This part introduces important IFS concepts and guiding principles that you'll need to understand before embarking on your parts work journey. Also included here are grounding skills and awareness-building activities to help prepare you mentally and emotionally for this undertaking. These skills and activities are designed to help you build a strong foundation to support your IFS practice.

CHAPTER ONE

The Internal Family Systems Model

This chapter offers a comprehensive overview of the IFS approach, the evidence-based model of psychotherapy created more than 40 years ago by Dr. Richard C. Schwartz. The practice is no longer limited to the realm of psychotherapy, however. The organizations that evolved around it—the IFS Institute and the Foundation for Self Leadership—now offer training and support globally to many types of practitioners, programs, and organizations. Together, they are carrying out the joint mission of bringing emotional, relational, and societal healing, and in turn, greater Self-energy, to the world. Here, you will gain a more detailed understanding of the model's components and how they all fit together.

A New Model of the Mind

When first introduced to the IFS approach, many clients I've worked with ask, "Does this mean I have multiple personality disorder or something?" This response is quite understandable, as most of us have grown up with the notion that we have an indivisible and unitary mind that contains the thoughts, emotions, memories, impulses, and images we experience. Based on this belief, our thoughts, emotions, and behaviors are viewed as reflections of who we are—and those that are socially unacceptable are a challenge to our core identity. When this occurs, we tend to try to suppress or control these aspects of ourselves, usually resulting in the feeling that we are somehow damaged or flawed.

In *No Bad Parts*, Dr. Schwartz points out, "The mono-mind paradigm has caused us to fear our parts and view them as pathological. In our attempts to control what we consider to be disturbing thoughts and emotions, we just end up fighting, ignoring, disciplining, hiding, or feeling ashamed of those impulses that keep us from doing what we want to do in our lives. And then we shame ourselves for not being able to control them." An example of this is when someone is labeled "an angry person" for expressing their anger. Even if a person experiences extreme anger at times, that does not reflect the entirety of who they are. And yet, many people equate who they are with what they feel, think, or do, leading them to try to control or eliminate such "problematic" responses. This can then result in further disconnection from oneself and others. Many of our feeling states and thought patterns are needlessly characterized as abnormal in this way—anxiety, persistent sadness, insecurity, and addictive tendencies, to name a few. They can become a stigmatizing identifier for the whole person if we remain in this mono-mind perspective.

Thankfully, the tide has begun to turn with regard to how we view ourselves. The mono-mind perspective was challenged somewhat by psychoanalyst Carl Jung and others who recognized and worked to normalize some form of subpersonalities within. More recently, evidence of this has also arisen in our popular culture—for example, the 2015 Disney-Pixar film *Inside Out* encourages us to "meet the little voices" inside our head, and singer-songwriter Alanis Morissette expresses something of her own internal work in her song "Empathy" when she writes about her hidden and denied parts. IFS is currently being utilized not only in places like psychotherapy offices, treatment centers, and college campuses, but also in public schools and medical centers, work with veterans, in corporate settings, and as a way to assist those impacted by war and societal conflicts.

Your Internal Family

Let's consider the nature of the Self, the network of parts that surround it, and the differences in our internal experience when Self is in the lead or when our parts take over that position.

Self: An Agent for Healing

Self exists in all of us. It is undamaged, cannot be wounded, and has an innate ability to offer healing. We tend to feel Self-energy in those times of flow, or being in the zone, when everything feels in balance, harmonious, and natural, and we experience a sense of wholeness and ease. Many people describe it as their "core" or "true Self" and know intuitively that it is a different entity than their parts, having a much broader perspective. There is the awareness that everything is connected both internally and externally. It shows up as a loving presence with inherent wisdom and a deeper knowing. In IFS work, it is known by its qualities, many of which begin with the letter "c":

- Curiosity
- Compassion
- Confidence
- Clarity
- Courage
- Creativity
- Calmness
- Connectedness

While these are the original 8 Cs used to describe Self, others have been added, including *constant*, *centered*, *spacious*, *intuitive*, *active*, *embodied*, and *offering choice*. As internal healer, the Self also tends to express at least five other qualities, which all happen to start with the letter "p":

- Presence
- Patience
- Perspective
- Persistence
- Playfulness

Self has the capacity to act as a supportive vessel for all of our parts, including their feelings and their experiences, and is able to hold and bear witness to their struggles and pain with compassion and love. As we all know, a state of flow tends to be fleeting, no matter how hard we may try to hold on to it. For this reason, it's helpful to think of accessing our Self-energy as a process and not necessarily a destination. This is actually why many people refer to their IFS work as a life practice. With awareness, we keep noticing the dance of our parts stepping forward to do their important work and the presence of Self to hold, support, and offer perspective from a more wholistic standpoint.

Different Types of Parts

There are really only two kinds of parts: the protectors and those they protect, the exiles, which are our vulnerable parts. All our parts have positive intentions for us, though it may not appear that way at first glance. Within the protector realm, there are two distinct "camps" that can be recognized by the ways in which they carry out their roles.

The first group are our *managers*, the ones that help us handle our daily lives, and are *proactive* in their attempts to accomplish this. Their goal is to try to keep us in control of situations and relationships to protect the vulnerable parts from experiencing any additional sense of humiliation, hurt, or rejection. A motto our managers live by is generally "never again," and this group includes our perfectionistic and achiever parts, anxious worriers, skeptical and doubting parts, our inner critics and judges, analyzing and intellectual "thinking" parts, caretakers and people-pleasers, passive-pessimists, and risk-avoidant parts. Their mission is to *prevent* further harm from entering the internal system in whatever way they can. They might show up to us as particular thought patterns or voices we hear in or around our head, a tightening or discomfort in the chest or throat, or certain images that illustrate who they are and what they endeavor to do for us.

The second group is known as the *firefighters*, whose motto is "fight fire with fire." These are the heroic, reactive, and impulsive first responders on the scene when the pain of our vulnerable parts has somehow been activated. They rush in to douse the emotional fires that have ignited internally with whatever they think will work. They have little concern for consequences, often engaging in behaviors intended to numb or avoid the pain. Alternatively, they will find ways to distract us and dissociate until the fire dies out. Common firefighters include our angry parts, our rebels, those that distract (e.g., by overworking or binging on screen time), and those that soothe or check out with alcoholic drinks or other substances (including food and money). They can also manifest in more extreme ways, depending on the degree of internal distress. This can be the result of past traumatic experiences and can show up as addictions, rage, self-harm, panic attacks, sexual acting out, or severe dissociation.

While these heightened expressions of firefighter behavior are less socially acceptable and often extremely problematic, they are also usually quite misunderstood. Our firefighters actually prefer to take on new roles once they are assured that the danger of emotional overwhelm is being attended to. Awareness of our firefighters comes by noticing the behavior patterns connected to particular urges or knee-jerk reactions inside, often with a revved-up feeling or the desire to shut down or escape. When we get to know and understand the firefighters better, they will often show us an image of themselves or will help us recognize how they manifest uniquely in our bodies.

This brings us to our most innocent, vulnerable, sensitive, and intimacy-loving parts, the ones that are *being* protected. They are called *exiles*. These are the young ones inside who've experienced what feels to be immense hurt and possibly trauma. Typically, they are kept out of our awareness for their own and the system's safety because the protectors fear that their emotional burdens will overwhelm and render us unable to function. Examples of our exiles are parts that feel abandoned, undeserving, dependent, unworthy, guilty, shameful, hopeless, unlovable, fearful or terrified, and grief-stricken, to name a few.

These parts can become increasingly extreme in their efforts to be witnessed, cared for, and listened to. Wounded exiles are the ones that both absorbed and continue to carry hefty emotional loads. Exiles often make themselves known to us through the body, such as an ache or heaviness in the chest or around the heart, a pain or sick feeling in the gut, deep sadness and the urge to cry, feeling shut down or isolated, or despairing and self-blaming thought patterns.

Living in Harmony

In IFS work, our intent is to tap into as much Self-energy as possible so that we have greater access to *all* of who we truly are and can then live from a place of authenticity, balance, and wholeheartedness. As a consistent IFS practice progresses, our parts do become more trusting that Self is available and able to *lead* the system, and this trust comes as a direct response to Self's awareness and appreciation of the challenges, worries, and hard work that parts are engaged in on our behalf. Such trust unfolds over time as we continue to acknowledge the depths of our parts' commitment to their work and gently offer the *hope* that when the system is ready, the metaphorical ropes that keep them tied to these demanding roles might loosen up or be released altogether. As systemic healing progresses, our parts can come to embody Self-energy as well.

When Self can be more present and *connected* to parts on a daily basis, offering a safe and nonjudgmental spaciousness inside that encourages the full expression of all parts' concerns, needs, and fears, we begin to live in greater harmony. Establishing such collaborative and compassionate relationships, not only *between* Self and parts, but *among* parts as well, is truly the key to this work. It brings with it the recognition that even our most challenging parts are inherently valuable and deserve our attention and care. This is actually what is meant by the IFS assurance that "all parts are welcome." As Tom Holmes puts it in *Parts Work*, we are "cultivating the capacity to be present and calm through a difficult process or experience" as we attend to our parts every day. So, our practice—and challenge—is to keep coming back to Self as the reassuring and constant "center" from which to live our lives.

For a visual representation of the internal family system, take a look at the IFS mandala in figure 1. This mandala was conceived and designed by senior IFS clinician and mentor Janet R. Mullen, LCSW, who reflects

The Internal Family System Mandala

Text adapted from *Internal Family Systems Therapy*, 1st ed., by Dr. Richard C. Schwartz; used with permission from mandala creator Janet R. Mullen, LCSW.

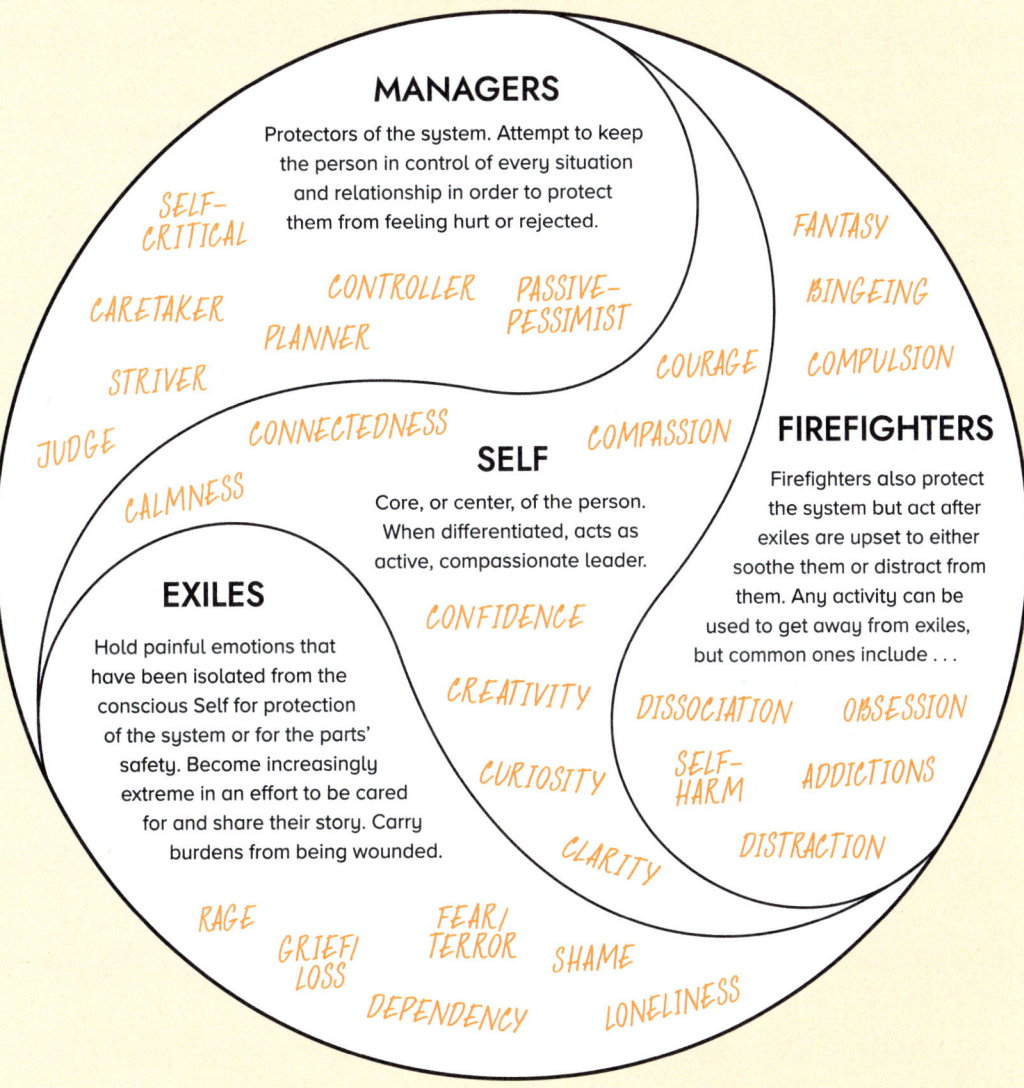

MANAGERS

Protectors of the system. Attempt to keep the person in control of every situation and relationship in order to protect them from feeling hurt or rejected.

SELF-CRITICAL

CARETAKER

PLANNER

CONTROLLER

PASSIVE-PESSIMIST

STRIVER

JUDGE

CONNECTEDNESS

CALMNESS

SELF

Core, or center, of the person. When differentiated, acts as active, compassionate leader.

COURAGE

COMPASSION

FANTASY

BINGEING

COMPULSION

FIREFIGHTERS

Firefighters also protect the system but act after exiles are upset to either soothe them or distract from them. Any activity can be used to get away from exiles, but common ones include . . .

EXILES

Hold painful emotions that have been isolated from the conscious Self for protection of the system or for the parts' safety. Become increasingly extreme in an effort to be cared for and share their story. Carry burdens from being wounded.

CONFIDENCE

CREATIVITY

CURIOSITY

CLARITY

DISSOCIATION

OBSESSION

SELF-HARM

ADDICTIONS

DISTRACTION

RAGE

GRIEF/LOSS

FEAR/TERROR

SHAME

DEPENDENCY

LONELINESS

Figure 1. A visual depiction of the Internal Family System

Coming Home to Self—Spiritual Connections

When people ask me what Self is, I often explain that, for me, Self is the divine spark within each of us; it is that which connects us to one another and to the greater Self-energy that's out there within the context of whatever belief system we might have. All the major faith traditions and spiritual paths echo the same basic belief that our core essence is naturally patient, loving, and kind, or as Dr. Schwartz writes in an article for *Psychotherapy Networker* magazine, "We are sparks of the eternal flame, manifestations of the absolute ground of being" and "it exists in all of us, just below the surface of our extreme parts." The poet, mystic, and theologian Thomas Merton put it this way in *Conjectures of a Guilty Bystander*: "It is in everybody, and if we could see it we would see billions of points of light coming together in the face and blaze of a sun that would make all the darkness and cruelty of life vanish completely . . . if only everyone could realize this! But it cannot be explained. There is no way of telling people that they are all walking around shining like the sun."

The divine can be known by any number of names (e.g., Source, the Inner Light, the Great Spirit, the Beloved, or the Higher Self). Such loving presence can be invited along on your healing journey. It may organically surface as you practice accessing your Self-energy. Longtime IFS senior trainer Michi Rose, PhD, once spoke to this in a personal communication: "The Self is our link to the Source; [it] opens us to be fully who we are. To access the Self is to access the Source. Although it seems as if the unlimited is outside of us and enters into us through the Self, in another sense we are already unlimited within. The Source is already inside of us. We only need to awaken within. The Self *is* the Source."

in a personal communication that she created it to show the flowing nature of Self's presence in the center "touching all areas and yet surrounded by them." She goes on to say, "I see our internal system as amazingly vast—a brilliant, wise and expansive system of energy rooted in love." This illustration has been a widely used symbol for teaching the IFS model for many years, both as a visual way to depict it and as a blueprint to create a personalized parts map (which you will have an opportunity to try later).

A System in Disequilibrium

Because our internal workings are a complex set of interactions and relationships that we generally haven't paid much attention to, much less learned to approach with openheartedness, our exiles are carrying heavy burdens from the past. Our protectors are determined to continue to do what they've always done to keep those exiles safely secluded from our awareness. They do this out of a sincere belief that it is the only way to avoid emotional overwhelm. Let's consider what happens when there is this kind of dynamic in the system and why.

When Parts Blend

The term "blending" is used in IFS to help us understand what happens when our parts feel the need to merge their impulses, beliefs, and emotions with the Self in order to do their jobs most effectively. This is a spontaneous process, and when it occurs, the part that has blended is considered to be leading the system. This is often helpful, as our parts assist us in countless ways as we live our lives. However, when they feel the need to do this in response to stressful or difficult external circumstances, we often don't realize that a part has taken the lead. In fact, it can feel as though we *are* that part. For example, when we become annoyed by someone or something, it can feel all-consuming, as though this annoyance is all there is. Similarly, such blending can happen with many other feeling states, such as anxiety, sadness, worry, impatience, or feeling judgmental or critical.

Our parts blend with the Self because it is their way of assuring our safety, the mission that our protectors are most committed to, and this may feel completely normal to us until we've learned to bring awareness to the process. As is true for most of what goes on in our internal worlds, the degree to which our parts blend with the Self exists on a continuum. As mentioned, we may not even notice that a part is in charge, or we may feel so completely overtaken by it that we have difficulty functioning.

It helps to remember here that our protectors fully believe that if they don't take over this way something awful will happen, so they really feel that they have no choice. Because these parts usually had to activate at an early age to protect us in some way, they do not yet have the whole story; they think we are still young as well and that we don't yet have the resources we need to deal with the situations that arise, or even to survive. Until they can be shown otherwise, these parts will usually stick determinedly to their agenda.

Such devotion is costly, however, as our protectors become weighed down by years of functioning this way, since remaining anxious, critical, or worried is quite exhausting. While our exiles bear the wounds from the past, our protectors are often burdened as well, though this may not be readily apparent given their highly focused approach to fulfilling their duties. They will frequently admit to feeling quite constrained by fatigue due to their chronic state of hyper-responsibility or vigilance, as well as feeling misunderstood and unappreciated for their hard work.

Sometimes our parts blend so fully that they become what we call "Self-like" parts. These parts resemble Self because they can appear to have some of the qualities of Self, but they lack the full healing capacity that

Self brings to the system. Because these parts masquerade as Self and can therefore be tricky to identify initially, it is important to be aware of them, along with ways to distinguish them from Self. I will discuss this further in chapter 4, but for now, it is helpful to know that as subtle as they may be, our Self-like parts *always* have some sort of agenda, either for the system overall or for a particular part we may be trying to work with. Other parts can feel when a Self-like part is standing in Self's place, and we may, in turn, feel stuck or worry that the IFS process isn't working. This is a common occurrence, as it really does take time for all our parts, including the "Self-like" ones, to trust us enough to truly relax and allow Self to lead.

Parts in Extreme Roles

Because our parts don't realize at first that there is a Self that can lead the system and attend to their needs, they often take on extreme roles to carry out their important work. In response to the lack of awareness our parts have that they are *not* completely on their own, I frequently use a metaphor in which Self is the sun and parts are the clouds. If we did not know or believe that the sun is present on a totally cloudy day, when we can't see it, we would likely be convinced that there is no sun.

When all our parts can see are the clouds, or other parts, of course they assume that there is no Self. Without any meaningful *experience* of Self-energy, our parts think they're alone and locked into their roles. And they experience increased pressure inside when they sense that the stakes are high. They often feel that they had to take on roles that they dislike or are now fatigued by, but they also don't trust that they can truly be released from these roles. This is quite a bind for them and is precisely why they become extreme at times.

Our internal family system is composed of interdependent relationships among our parts. They tend to be highly reactive to one another, much like in an external family in conflict, creating strong alliances and polarizations among themselves. Along the lines of Newton's third law of motion, which states that "every action has an equal and opposite reaction," the more extreme one part of the system becomes, another part or parts react in an equally if not more extreme way. We often see such polarizations play out between our managers and firefighters, but they occur with exiles as well.

Other reasons our parts remain in these extreme roles include the need to protect other parts, usually heavily burdened exiles. One thing that contributes to such high distress for the exiles is the fact that they are usually stuck in the past at the point when they were hurt and are quite alone. They don't have any awareness that circumstances have changed or feel much hope for themselves. An additional factor to consider is that something in our external environment may be activating the system, and this may even result in a cluster of parts becoming more intense than they might otherwise be. I'll discuss many of these issues in more detail later, but having some awareness of them is necessary as we consider the whole IFS process next.

The IFS Process

Before setting off on any substantial journey, it's always helpful to get the lay of the land. Let's take a comprehensive look at the IFS process, including its goals, along with the option to invite a supportive helper to join you for part of the experience.

The Goals of IFS Therapy

There are four primary goals of IFS therapy based on the model's assumptions, concepts, and methods designed to bring greater understanding and transformation to the internal system. They are:

1. **Help to free parts from their extreme roles:** This goal focuses on unblending from and eventually unburdening parts so that they can all become less constrained by emotional burdens and can then choose more preferred roles within the system.

2. **Restore trust in the Self and its ability to lead the system:** This points to the importance of establishing enduring Self-to-part relationships, beginning with Self's acknowledgment of and gratitude for how hard parts are working, and compassionate recognition of their wounding.

3. **Work toward greater harmony, balance, and wholeness:** The focus here is on the systemic nature of relationships among parts, so that once they are known and Self-energy becomes more available to them, they can get along better as a whole with less conflict. This goal applies outwardly as well, as it also assists our parts to express themselves and to engage in relationships and external situations in more balanced ways.

4. **Cultivate Self-energy in the external world:** As we progress on the path of understanding and offering healing to our own parts, we have greater capacity to extend this to not only our own relationships and social circles but also to the world at large.

Step-by-Step IFS

Before we delve into what is involved in the IFS process, it is important to remember that there are a few differences between practicing IFS on your own and working with an IFS therapist. As noted earlier, the first is that the deep unburdening work with your exiles, which is often a cornerstone of the work with an IFS therapist, will *not* be included here for safety reasons. With that one exception, IFS therapists use the same step-by-step approach to this work that you will be guided through here.

Another key difference is that when you work with an IFS therapist, two "Selves" are available to you—your own and the therapist's. This is especially helpful and necessary when approaching the often-intense work of helping our exiles (and other highly triggered parts) to unburden. However, it can be helpful at other times as well; sometimes we all need to borrow a bit of Self-energy from a caring, supportive, and nonjudgmental helper until we can regain our connection to our own Self-energy.

Another distinction is that in practicing IFS on your own, you will be following your own "inner compass," which means you can take all the time you need to prepare for and engage in the process. You won't need to attend to the parts of you that might worry about not meeting someone else's expectations or about getting it right. While an IFS therapist will make it clear that there is no rush, practicing on your own allows you to fully explore your inner landscape at your own pace.

As you'll see in the following description, IFS distinguishes between our work with protectors and exiles by what they *do* within the system— basically our protectors have a *job* to accomplish, whereas our exiles have a *story* to tell. Another difference between them is that exiles are usually stuck in the past, but our protectors, despite having come on board at an early age, live in the here and now. Because of their gate-keeper role, protectors are our key to entering the system. They carry a wealth of knowledge about the history and understanding of the exiles' pain and the entrenched relational dynamics, therefore, much of our work needs to focus on them.

WORKING WITH PROTECTIVE PARTS

There are some important goals in IFS for working with our protectors. While there can be a couple of differences depending on whether the focus is on a manager or a firefighter, the overall goals are:

1. Establish a Self-to-part relationship through the unblending process to *build trust* in the Self.

2. Get to know this part as fully as possible and address its fears.

3. Request permission from the part to talk with either the exile this part protects or another part you'd like to work with.

4. Determine whether this protector would like to and might now feel able to shift into a less extreme role.

5. Offer Self-energy throughout the system to facilitate a greater sense of harmony within the inner family.

In order to begin to meet these goals with our protectors, we follow a six-step process known as the 6 Fs. They are:

1. **Find** a part or parts: We begin the process here by first turning our attention inward and really *noticing* what we are feeling or experiencing in the moment. This may come as words or thoughts, bodily sensations, emotions, or images.

2. **Focus** on this part: As we concentrate on whatever is arising inside, we take time to begin to recognize whether this part would like our attention now.

3. **Flesh** out the "target" part: Assuming we have decided the feeling, sensation, thought, or image is a part we'd like to work with, we ask it to provide more information about itself so that we can have a clearer sense of who it is; we listen closely to what it wants us to know about itself and ask it to show itself to us more completely.

4. How do you **Feel** toward this part? This is a crucial point in the process as the answer to this question reveals whether or not Self is present with the part, or if there are other parts reacting

to it (hint: there usually are!). We spend whatever time we need to here unblending from reactive parts so that we can regain our access to Self and truly begin to establish a "Self-to-part" relationship.

5. **BeFriend** the target part: Once we have Self-energy on board, we express our curiosity and compassion toward the part, asking to learn more about what it does for us and how it came to be in this role, how old it is, what it tries to accomplish for us in this role, etc.

6. Ask the target part about its **Fears**: This step is also very important as it gives us a lot of information about what is keeping the part in its role. Here, we usually ask some version of "What do you think would happen if you weren't doing this job, or even if you took a break from it sometimes?"

We'll look at each step more closely in chapter 3, but for now, it's helpful to know that these steps are often grouped together and help guide our first meetings with our parts. The purpose of this six-step process is to initiate and cultivate trust in the relationship, allowing each part to experience Self in a tangible way.

WORKING WITH EXILES

In *No Bad Parts*, Dr. Schwartz explains that "originally the word heal meant 'to make whole' or 'to save.'" This is precisely the primary goal in working with our exiles, as helping them heal not only serves to restore them to a state of wholeness and vitality but also brings this healing to the entire internal system. More specifically, general goals for working with exiles are:

1. Once granted permission from its protector, allow the exile to *feel* Self's presence, care, and compassion, and allow as much

time and space as needed by the exile to feel a sense of trust and safety.

2. Fully listen, witness, and validate the exile's story, offering reassurance that the pain connected to that story can safely be released when, and only when, the exile is ready.

3. Empower the exile to choose when and how to unburden the pain it carries, whether or not it needs to be retrieved from the past, and whether or not it needs Self's assistance to attend to anything keeping it tethered to the past.

4. Facilitate the unburdening process and then assist the exile to become reintegrated in the internal family. (See step six on page 34 for more on reintegration.)

Even though you will not be guided to work with the unburdening process here, it is helpful to be aware of the steps involved. They are:

1. **Establish a Self-to-part relationship:** This involves slowing things down enough to be as fully present as possible with the exile in order to build trust, respectfully requesting that it not overwhelm the system and asking that both it and other parts, which might be reacting to it, unblend enough so that Self can stay with the exile.

2. **Understand and witness the story fully:** This is the opportunity the exile has been waiting for to feel completely seen and heard the way that it needed (but didn't get) at the time the hurtful event occurred.

3. **Retrieve the part from the past and/or assist it there if needed:** Some parts need help to come out of the painful scene in the past and into the present with Self, as well as to possibly "redo" the difficult events from the past internally to empower the exile.

4. **Help the part unburden its pain and negative beliefs:** Once the exile feels safe and its story has been fully witnessed, Self guides it through a symbolic internal ritual of unloading the burden, offering it the choice of how to do so, and lovingly assists it with this process in whatever way it needs.

5. **Invite the part to bring in qualities it wants to reclaim or needs now that the burden has been released:** This often happens spontaneously and allows the part to invite back into its body the things that it lost when it absorbed the burden or new qualities that it chooses for itself now.

6. **Help the unburdened exile reintegrate into the internal family:** This involves updating other parts, particularly this exile's protectors, about the healing that has just occurred and checking to see if any protectors would now like to unburden as well. Self checks for reactivity to these changes throughout the system and addresses concerns while also determining ways in which this exile would like continued contact with Self.

Unburdening is a powerful experience that requires Self to be continually present at every stage of the process; it is also a time when emotions can feel overwhelming and protector parts can easily blend with Self. This is why you are not encouraged to engage in this process in this book. It is not because it isn't possible to do on your own but because it is most safely done with a therapist who can assist with the frequent unblending and requests that the exile not overwhelm the system that may be necessary. You will likely encounter your exiles along the way, however, and I'll offer guidance for being present with them when that occurs.

Understanding Your Psyche

In IFS, Self is considered our "seat of consciousness," the place from which we become aware of our parts and all we experience. So, from this seat of Self, the contents of our consciousness appear—what we perceive in the world around us and what goes on in our inner world where emotions, memories, and ideas arise. It is also from this place that we come to have some notion of our deeper subconscious functioning. In this sense, then, Self is that in us that has the ability to both contain and witness everything, inside and out. But unlike the somewhat "visible" internal workings of our parts, the Self is not actually seen but can be felt by our parts when we welcome them in.

There are many ways to think about our psyches in these terms, and numerous metaphors are used in IFS to help illustrate this principle. I find two of them particularly useful. The first is imagining our consciousness as a theater stage upon which our parts play out their internal dramas and in which Self is an active presence. The other is a castle metaphor, which depicts our protectors as the guards, either waiting to jump into action or busily devising preventive strategies to safeguard the fortress. Meanwhile, our exiles are either secured in a tower or the dungeon. The Self is seen as the benign sovereign who doesn't always feel available to many of the protectors and exiles but is ever present.

Sample Session: I Meet Some of My Parts

To give you an idea of how a Self-led IFS session might play out, this example illustrates what it is like to become aware of and have a dialogue with our parts as they show up inside as physical sensations, thoughts, voices we hear, visual images, memories, and so on. It is important to know that it is quite likely it will take a bit of time for your parts to warm up to the idea of you coming to be present with them in this way (since they haven't really experienced this before).

You may also find yourself feeling somewhat skeptical about the process. This is common, as many people have the initial sense that they are "making all this up." As you read the interaction I have with two of my parts, see if you can just notice any of the parts of *you* that might have these kinds of reactions. If it feels right to you, offer them a little reassurance. As Dr. Schwartz notes in *No Bad Parts*, "Why would you want to converse with thoughts and emotions? They can't talk back, can they? Well, it turns out that they can. In fact, they have a lot of important things to tell us." Exactly!

For this session, I've decided to explore my frequent desire to snack at night and the frustration I feel concerning this habit. To begin, I take a couple of deep breaths, settle into a comfortable space, and close my eyes to better notice what I'm feeling in my body as I think about this desire.

I'm aware of a tightness in my belly that feels a little uncomfortable and familiar, so as I focus on it, I ask myself how I feel toward it. Right away, I sense an annoyance toward it; I decide to start with that, which I'm experiencing as a voice in my head.

TANIS (T): "I'm hearing loud and clear that you're annoyed with that feeling in my stomach. Can you tell me more?"

ANNOYED PART (A): "Of course! That's the one that's been making you eat ice cream almost every night lately. It's getting out of hand!"

I quickly ask myself how I feel toward this part. I find that I actually am quite open to hearing more.

T: "I understand this is very upsetting for you; what else do you want me to know?"

A: "Yes, it is becoming a big problem; you know that you can't continue this, right? Having ice cream every night is so bad for you, and I think it sometimes numbs you out, so I feel like this behavior is out of control."

T: "Well, it's understandable that you're feeling this way; it sounds like you're just trying to protect me. Is that right?"

A: "Of course I am, and you need to get it to stop!"

T: "I totally get it, but what do you think might happen if we don't get the ice-cream eating under control?"

A: "I think that numbing thing will happen more frequently so that you'll be checked out *more* often

and won't be able to accomplish what you need to do."

T: "It makes sense that you'd be worried about that, but maybe we could see what this is really about. Would that be all right?"

A: "I guess so . . . but you have to make sure that the numbing doesn't take over."

As the Annoyed part says this, I feel the tightness in my belly again.

T: "I really appreciate your willingness to let me find out about this, and I'm certain we can do this in a way that it won't take over."

A: "OK, but I'm going to hang out in the background and watch, just to make sure."

T: "That's perfectly fine as long as you do your best to not interrupt as I work with this other part, OK?"

A: "Yes, I'll do my best."

Now I focus more on that sensation in my stomach, and again ask myself how I feel toward it. I notice I now feel quite curious about it.

T: "I'm definitely feeling you there in my belly, and I'd like to get to know you if that would be all right?"

I feel the tightening sensation ease up just a bit.

T: "It seems like you relaxed a little just now. Is there anything you could let me know about yourself or what you're trying to do in there? It doesn't have to be in words; you could show me in some way, or even just one word or phrase to help me understand you better."

I suddenly have a memory of when I was a kid and my mom let me have ice cream sometimes after school.

BELLY PART (B): "Let go."

T: "Oh, I see you just showed me when I'd be with Mom at the kitchen table after school having some ice cream. Can you let me know more about the scene or the phrase 'Let go'?"

B: "Sometimes it just feels good."

T: "You're right, it does. Would you help me understand what you're trying to do for me now, though, by getting me to have ice cream at night?"

B: "I'm just so tired of all the stress and how hard things can feel sometimes. It feels like we never get a break."

T: "That makes sense. So, it sounds like you're just trying to help me relax and slow down at night, right?"

B: "Well, yeah. You don't seem to be able to do it on your own because there are continual demands, and then sometimes when you stop you just feel really alone."

T: "Hmm . . . so are you trying to help with that, too?"

B: "Of course! This way you can feel better and not be lonely."

T: "OK, it's starting to make even more sense to me now. I know it should probably be obvious to me, but could you tell me what you're concerned would happen if you didn't persuade me to have ice cream at night?"

B: "The lonely one would take over, and if that happened, you probably wouldn't even make it to work the next day because you'd feel so bad."

T: "Well, I can certainly understand why you'd be worried, and I do appreciate that you've been trying to take care of me this way. Could you explain somehow who that lonely one is?"

The memory of me as a second grader at the kitchen table eating ice cream reappears.

T: "OK, got it. Thank you so much for showing me and for your vigilance to protect me. Would it be all right if I check in with you again, like maybe even at night when all this starts?"

B: "Yeah, but that doesn't mean I'll stop."

T: "I know, but I would like to get better acquainted with you and the Annoyed one, because I can see now how hard you both are working on my behalf. Would that be OK?"

B: "Yeah, I guess . . ."

T: "How about you, Annoyed one?"

A: "OK, but I still feel like this needs to stop."

T: "I know. I so appreciate you both. Let's keep talking about it."

CHAPTER TWO

Fundamental Skills and Exercises

In preparation for your IFS journey, this chapter provides some background on the body's responses to stress and trauma. Because the nervous system drives our body's responses to both safety and threat, this chapter delves into the nature of the nervous system to give you a firmer understanding of what happens on a physiological level and how that affects our thoughts and feelings. Following those discussions is a collection of skills and exercises to help you build your awareness and self-understanding, as well as your ability to take good care of yourself throughout this process.

How the Body Responds to Stress

The World Health Organization defines stress as "a state of worry or mental tension caused by a difficult situation," that is a "natural human response that prompts us to address challenges and threats in our lives." The fight-or-flight *energy* we feel in our bodies as a result is known as the stress response. It involves both psychological and physical reactions based on our perception of the potential impact of these situations. By definition, then, our experience of stress is both a state of being and an energy that is linked to how we perceive our circumstances or events. It is clearly an instinctual mind-body expression of the drive to keep ourselves safe and to take appropriate action to meet difficulties our bodies perceive to be threatening.

When we experience stress, our bodies react in ways that we generally miss unless they are extreme responses. In *Body Sense*, Alan Fogel, PhD, states that such "loss of attention to ourselves brings with it additional losses. We risk losing our emotional equanimity, our physical health, and our sense of well-being." That's a lot to lose, but this is exactly what often happens: after years of enduring and not attending to the fallout from chronic stress, many people develop physical and mental difficulties with no apparent cause, at least not within the standard Western medical approach.

In a social context that promotes thinking our way through challenges, the body is viewed as an object and not the subject of our experience; we have been socialized to ignore it when it speaks to us, especially when we're under stress. At those times, we can become so caught up in judgment, expectations, and external demands, that we often neglect our internal functioning. Bo Forbes, PsyD, describes this beautifully in *Bo's Guide: How to Survive + Thrive in 2022*: "Due to a cultural mindset that privileges the mind and marginalizes the body, we are a disembodied culture. We live in our heads." And while our heads can be particularly helpful, our emotions and our intuition, along with our parts and Self-energy, originate and express themselves as sensations *in* the body. Tuning into our internal experience ("felt sense") is vitally important—the body is where our parts and Self live.

While the body and nervous system are designed to handle small doses of stress quite well, managing intense or chronic stress can be problematic. Everyone's ability to effectively tolerate and work through the effects of stress is different, and depends on many individual characteristics, including one's temperament and personality traits. So, while some people are naturally more able to manage stress, others are much more sensitive and reactive to it. Both internal and external factors play a part in this process, as does the impact of trauma in a person's life.

Whether or not we realize it, we all have personal histories of dealing with trauma, which we may have worked through in some way or needed to suppress. There are many ways to define "trauma"; it is the Greek word for "wound," and it is generally thought to be the psychological or emotional response to an event or series of events or experiences that causes significant distress. In his foreword to Peter Levine's book *In an Unspoken Voice*, Dr. Gabor Maté writes, "Trauma is caused when we are unable to release blocked energies to fully move through the physical and emotional reactions to hurtful experiences."

Any type of psychologically distressing experience can result in lasting emotional impact. This is true whether a person experiences "big-T" trauma, which refers to major life-threatening or debilitating experiences such as natural disasters, sexual abuse, domestic violence, war, etc.; or "little-t" trauma, which can occur in response to difficult life events such as divorce, loss through death or estrangement, chronic financial stress, family conflict, job loss, or serious health issues. In *When the Past Is Always Present*, Ronald Ruden, MD, notes that the event "does not have to be life-threatening and must have significant meaning to the person that is linked to loss of attachments, relationships, status or life itself" in order to be traumatic.

According to Peter Levine, PhD, in *In an Unspoken Voice*, "Trauma is anything that our system can't handle or process. It is not what happens to us, but what we hold inside in the absence of an empathic witness." For example, when we are infants, if we are not fully attended to in times of distress we may become fearful that we won't survive. If we are held and soothed by an attuned caregiver (one who is aware of and receptive to our needs), we are restored to feeling safe and possibly even validated for our reactions. Such attunement is vital to both our physical and emotional development, but it is never perfect, no matter how much our caregivers try to consistently respond to our needs. As a result, we all end up internalizing some amount of emotional wounding that couldn't be fully addressed at the time the hurt occurred.

What ends up happening, as viewed through the IFS lens, is that these "unprocessed" responses get exiled in our developing internal family system, thereby contributing to the emotional burdens we carry.

Through the practice of IFS, we can learn to attend to our emotional wounds by being present to ourselves in the way we needed when the wounding first occurred. By accessing the Self, we can become our own empathic witness or attuned caregiver to our hurt parts. Mark Epstein, MD, sums this up nicely in *The Trauma of Everyday Life*: "If you create an atmosphere of attunement and responsiveness within yourself, one that mimics . . . the emotional state of an attentive parent, this pain and sorrow becomes not only endurable but self-liberating. It releases, and in the process, we can also be released." Learning to cultivate this healing state of presence and attunement—what we call Self-energy—is exactly what IFS is all about.

Getting to Know Your Nervous System

Developing an awareness of the particular nature of our own nervous systems is the first step in understanding how to consistently tap into this state of presence, or Self-energy. Basically, our autonomic nervous system (ANS) is hardwired for both safety and connection. It helps regulate many of the body's functions in an involuntary way well beyond our conscious awareness or control. In the article "A Beginner's Guide to Polyvagal Theory," Deb Dana, LCSW, trauma therapist and author, calls it our "personal surveillance system" in our "quest to feel safe in our bodies, our environments and in our relationships with others." This continual pursuit is primarily about survival, as we must rely on our connection with others in the external world, at least initially, not only to live but also to grow and thrive.

The difficulty is, however, that our nervous system did not evolve to be overstimulated or chronically triggered, as is often the case in our lives today. For this reason, it can be quite challenging for us to understand why we sometimes might have trouble both reaching and maintaining a state of presence. Let's take a look now at our body's ancient system of "survival intelligence" and the ways in which it correlates with the workings of our internal family system.

The autonomic nervous system contains two primary branches, the sympathetic and the parasympathetic. The sympathetic branch mobilizes us to take action when a threat is detected; this is the classic fight-or-flight response that fuels feelings of anxiety, anger, and fear, and tenses our muscles as adrenaline and other hormones pump into the body, energizing it to act quickly.

The second branch, the parasympathetic, is composed of two pathways that work to balance this activated energy in the system. It is associated with the rest-and-digest functions. These two channels are found in the vagus nerve, which is the longest cranial nerve. It begins at the base of the skull just behind the ears. It serves as a two-directional superhighway, extending down through the lungs, heart, diaphragm, and stomach, and back upward through both sides of the neck, throat, eyes, and ears. The most important nerve in the body, the vagus nerve delivers information back and forth from the brain to the body and back from the body to the brain about pain, temperature changes, heart rate, blood pressure, and gut sensations.

Running along the back of the vagus nerve is the dorsal vagal pathway, which responds to cues of extreme danger or to excessive arousal in the sympathetic system. When such cues are detected, it shuts the body down into a state of "freeze." Normally, the dorsal vagal pathway performs the positive role of helping us modulate between states of arousal and relaxation, but if the system is too aroused, as can occur when a trauma or major stress response is triggered, it will activate, immobilizing us completely. We end up feeling checked out, disconnected, or numb, and often unable to communicate what we're feeling. Many people describe this experience as one of dissociation and even collapse.

At the front of the vagus nerve is the ventral vagal pathway. When this pathway is activated, we feel calm, connected to ourselves and others, clearheaded, balanced, and safe. When the ventral vagal pathway is active and attuned, we feel a sense of freedom and agency in the world. There is also more capacity to move fluidly from potentially triggered states of sympathetic or dorsal vagus nervous system arousal back to this place of emotional and physical regulation—or what we experience as flow. We are accessible to both ourselves and those around us when the ventral vagal system is dominant, and our bodies feel safe enough to express vulnerability because we can *trust* that we are supported and protected.

So, from a survival standpoint, our bodies are physiologically tuned to continually monitor, both internally and externally, for cues that lead to either defensive or trusting responses to one profound question: "Am I safe?" While these are primarily unconscious processes, you can learn to become more aware of the particular stress states and patterns in your own nervous system and consciously send your body signals of safety by utilizing some of the physical interventions found in the exercises at the end of this chapter. Our goal here is to create a safe container within the body involving enough Self-energy so that you'll be better able to recognize, tolerate, and work with these responses as you move through them.

It's also important to consider what happens when there is either too much arousal in the system or when activation has been shut down, and how this might correlate with our parts. When the sympathetic nervous system is overactivated, or hyperaroused, the message inside, again according to Deb Dana, LCSW, in the article mentioned earlier, is "move, take action, escape—no place is safe." Such "sympathetic mobilization" is all about protection from threat and results in feelings of anxiety, anger, overwhelm, the need to move, and the inability to focus or follow through due to the sense that the world is chaotic, dangerous, unfriendly, and can't be trusted. This is where certain protector parts spring into action as well, since they feel the need for *control* given such high activation. According to Ruth Culver, an IFS and trauma therapist and creator of the "Survive/Thrive Spiral" of trauma, these protector parts seek safety through *action* and follow the mantra "I must." Often referred to as "fix protectors," the traits and qualities they employ to do their jobs in this state include hypervigilance, anxiety, rebellion, perfectionism, rushing, impulsivity, overcontrolling, criticizing, hyperactivity, obsessive-compulsive behaviors, panic attacks, and rage.

On the other end of the spectrum is the dorsal vagal reaction to extreme stress or chronic hyperarousal, which is to freeze and shut down the system. This state is called hypoarousal. Safety here is sought through disconnection and submission, resulting in a sense of feeling very alone. This is exactly the experience of our exiles who feel helpless, hopeless, abandoned, and resigned. From this physiological place, we may isolate ourselves, experience brain fog and heavy fatigue, or become depressed, disconnected, and appeasing. We might also zone out, dissociate, and engage in numbing addictions with the help of our firefighters. The primary messages from our parts here are "I hurt" and "I can't" because they're often frozen in the past due to their unprocessed pain; this nervous system response of hypoarousal reflects the exiles' despair in a deep physical way.

Between these two states of extreme dysregulation is the state where we ideally spend most of our time—in *calm arousal*, when we feel relatively capable of handling the demands of our lives without much difficulty and can even reach that state of flow where we feel relaxed, balanced, and grounded. This state is also where Self-energy is most present, and it is from this position that we can most effectively handle day-to-day challenges and more flexibly move in and out of heightened

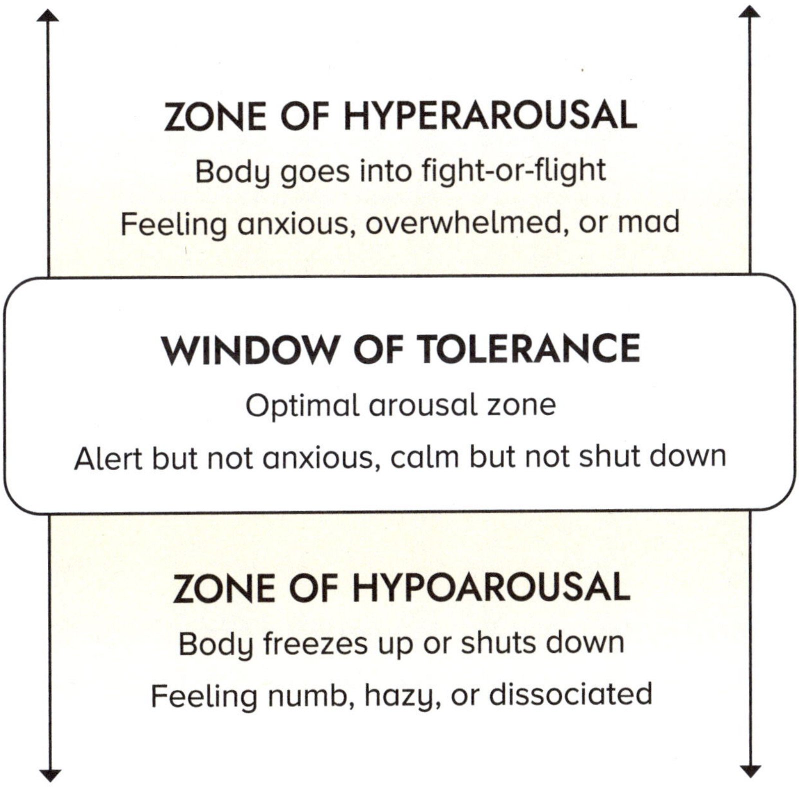

ZONE OF HYPERAROUSAL
Body goes into fight-or-flight
Feeling anxious, overwhelmed, or mad

WINDOW OF TOLERANCE
Optimal arousal zone
Alert but not anxious, calm but not shut down

ZONE OF HYPOAROUSAL
Body freezes up or shuts down
Feeling numb, hazy, or dissociated

Figure 2. Adapted from Siegel, D. (2009). *Mindsight: The New Science of Personal Transformation*. NSW, Australia. Scribe Publications.

emotional states. This is the place that Dr. Dan Siegel had in mind when he originated the concept of the "window of tolerance." This is illustrated in figure 2.

The size of this "window" is a bit different for all of us. It is seen as the optimal zone of emotional regulation and resilience from which we can live our most centered, functional, and satisfying lives. Since we recognize that it is unrealistic to expect to always remain in this spacious, Self-led place, the key is to become more aware of what our personal window for tolerating stress and activation might look like. This awareness can help us increase our capacity to return to it effectively when triggered.

We can practice noticing when our window of tolerance is expanded and wide. During these moments of spaciousness, we may feel comfortable and safe, and even if an obstacle is encountered, we can move through it with relative ease. We can also notice how our window of tolerance narrows and contracts when we encounter adversity, excessive stress, or trauma. As this occurs, we might feel more anxious, uncomfortable, and maybe even unsafe. If we can remember to breathe, reach out for help, and remain grounded in our bodies as much as possible during these moments, we can ride out the waves of dysregulation until we feel calm and our window widens again. This takes practice, of course, but the more we engage in the effort to expand our window of tolerance in this way, the more resilience we will experience.

You may feel challenged at various points as your IFS journey unfolds, so it can be extremely helpful to build your awareness of your personal window of tolerance. To do this, consider the difference between what you might experience as unsafe levels of stress (which could include feeling emotionally triggered, overwhelmed, wanting to shut down, or feeling stuck in a dissociative state) and the usual discomfort that can accompany an intense, but still safe, self-help process.

If something does feel unsafe to your system, it is critical to listen to your body's cues and your intuition. Take the necessary steps to care for yourself appropriately if you become overwhelmed. This might require slowing down or taking a break from this work, seeking the assistance of a qualified psychotherapist or other medical professional (depending on the severity and nature of your reaction), connecting with an empathic friend or loved one, or repeatedly doing the exercises at the end of this chapter. Many of the exercises are aimed at stimulating the vagus nerve to calm the stress response.

Because IFS is an embodied practice, involving work with our emotions that *begin* as sensations in the body, some amount of discomfort is to be expected. Bo Forbes, PsyD, expresses this beautifully in *Bo's Guide: How to Survive + Thrive in 2022*: "Naturally, entering the world of the body can be uncomfortable and intimidating . . . when we learn to attend to sensations, we become more comfortable with the discomfort. We expand the repertoire of sensations we can receive and tolerate. In time and with practice, the wilderness of the body feels like home. This is sensory resilience."

Factors That Affect Your Sense of Safety

Building sensory and emotional resilience serves as both a secure foundation from which to begin your IFS journey as well as a potential result of safely undertaking this deeply personal work. What might feel safe to one person in this process, however, may feel unsafe for someone else. Try to take stock of the external challenges to your sense of safety as well as those that are more internal for a clearer awareness of their impact on both your nervous system and your internal family system. Considering these factors may help support you in reducing certain stressors that could make engaging in this work more difficult for

Finding an IFS Therapist

While working through this book, you may wonder whether it would be beneficial for you to find a qualified IFS therapist to help you go deeper with your healing work. There are several resources available to assist you in this process.

The most comprehensive and easiest to navigate is the directory of trained IFS therapists and practitioners, which can be found on the Internal Family Systems Institute website at **IFS-Institute.com**. You can search their directory by location and find information on individual therapists and practitioners. Many do take insurance or sometimes offer sliding scale fees and list that as part of their profile. You can also see whether particular therapists are accepting new clients and what their areas of specialty are.

Another option is the IFS Telehealth Collective, which includes fully trained IFS therapists licensed to provide telehealth sessions in the states of California, Florida, Massachusetts, Michigan, New York, and Oregon. You can check them out at **IFSTherapyOnline.com**.

The Internal Family Systems Counselling Association based in Canada may be an option as well. Their website is **IFSCA.ca**. Most of the therapists who appear on this site are located in Canada, but some are located in the United States and other countries. Under the "directory" tab, you'll find therapists listed in different categories with full pages of information for each listing once you click on a name.

One other resource for finding a therapist can be found at IFS therapist Jenna Riemersma's website at **JennaRiemersma.com**. Under the "resources" tab on her site, Jenna includes a listing of Christian IFS therapists and links to their contact information and websites. The IFS therapists listed there generally do not only see Christian clients but offer a Christian perspective as an option in their work.

you. It may also prepare you to better recognize your unique patterns of activation in response to certain kinds of triggers.

First, let's look at potential concerns in your outer environment that might influence your sense of safety. These could include the amount of stress you experience in your job, the level of security you feel in your living situation or community, whether you're experiencing conflict in your relationships, the strength of your social support network, and financial issues or worries. This list doesn't cover every aspect of your life but will hopefully help you start thinking about whether or not you feel generally safe and protected in these and other areas. When you have a sense of potential triggers in your external world, you may be able to bring greater compassion to parts of you that are particularly reactive to them.

This holds true for internal challenges as well. Included here are things like the quality of your sleep and the ability to get enough rest, significant health issues or physical limitations, your personal experience with loss and trauma, and the degree to which you've been able to grieve and emotionally process these events. In addition, your *perceived* sense of safety (which may have to do with underlying anxiety, depression, or other psychological concerns) and the particular temperament you were born with are also important considerations.

Being a naturally sensitive person myself, I can attest to the powerful relationship between temperament and our internal family systems. Though our innate wiring (e.g., biological rhythms, adaptability, sensitivity, mood, and introversion versus extroversion) doesn't really change much with time, it can be influenced to some degree by our family, culture, and life experiences. When you have an awareness of these internal tendencies and influences, you are in a better position to attend to your unique needs when it comes to feeling secure in your relationships and generally satisfied in your life. It also helps you better understand and appreciate all your parts.

If you become overwhelmed or very triggered regarding your sense of safety at any time as you work through this book, again, it may be necessary to slow down or take a break. It is important to remember that your internal family system is all about protection and your parts are primed to react when things don't feel safe. It is also important to recognize the wisdom of this response. While it is sometimes hard to be patient with the slow pace of the IFS process, it is essential to respect the need for this. The reality is that our internal family systems will not allow us to do anything that doesn't feel right or safe until the parts feel a critical mass of Self-energy and trust. It takes time and consistent presence with your parts for this to develop. So, when your system becomes triggered, return to the grounding and calming exercises at the end of this chapter and build awareness through journaling for help.

The Healing Power of Your Awareness

When beginning to work with the IFS approach, awareness is the path we take to explore our inner world. By turning our attention inward, which we seldom do given all the daily external demands and distractions, it may initially feel difficult to slow down enough to really notice what's happening inside. Bringing a curious and compassionate awareness to the internal chatter, conflicting emotions, discomfort and tension, along with the wisdom and guidance inherent in our parts, is in itself an act of Self-leadership.

Being aware of and tuning into your parts is the first step toward bringing healing to the internal system. This is actually how you "get into Self" to do this work. To illustrate, let's say you happen to notice a nagging irritation buzzing in your head. Instead of trying to push it away, you decide instead to turn *toward* it inwardly to see if it's possible to just be curious about it and to even let that irritation know you are curious about it. As you listen closely, the irritation shares through words, thoughts, or images that it is upset because a good friend "just doesn't care." That person has been out of touch during a difficult time, and it doesn't understand why. Already a clearer picture emerges of this irritated part and what may be behind its concerns, and a dialogue between you (the Self) and this part has begun. "Awareness of a Part" on page 66 will help you begin to build such awareness and potentially meet one of your parts as your first step on this journey.

Parts and Our Relationships

Another aspect of becoming aware of our parts has to do with the ways in which they arise and impact our relationships with others. When noticing and talking about our parts in this context, our approach actually matters a great deal. One powerful tool that will also help you along your IFS journey is the practice of learning to speak *for* rather than *from* your parts. While this may not appear, at first, to be a very important distinction, it is actually a very significant one, as it enables us to work toward being more "Self-led" in our everyday lives with those we care about. This seemingly very simple strategy allows us to unblend from parts that become reactive in our interactions, thereby helping us to communicate *from Self* rather than from those parts.

So, here's how it works. Let's say I'm having lunch with a good friend and am in the middle of telling her about a difficult experience I had when she starts scrolling on her cell phone. Reacting *from* my very annoyed part might sound something like: "Don't let me interrupt you—I'm sure whatever is on your phone is more important than what I'm trying to tell you." Instead, I can take a breath and check inside with that annoyed one, reassuring it that I can speak *for* it, and then say: "I'm noticing a part of me that is annoyed that you're checking your phone while I was trying to tell you something important—is everything OK?" While doing this does take awareness, practice, and trust from our parts, we can see from this example what a difference it can make. We can actually stay more present *in* the interaction this way, as our parts can still feel heard but are not as likely to trigger a "parts-led" response from the other person. Practicing this skill can be both validating for our parts and an invitation to bring more compassion to our relationships.

Getting Grounded

What You'll Need

- 20 to 40 minutes of uninterrupted time
- A journal, sketchpad, or digital notebook
- Pen, colored pencils, or markers (if desired)
- A recording device (if desired)

Overview

Becoming more grounded physically, emotionally, and energetically is a powerful tool for connecting to Self-energy and learning to be more fully present in our bodies and in our internal systems. Because we want to start with both feet on the ground, it's important to reconnect our own energy to the earth to reestablish a sense of stability, calm the nervous system, and return to a centered place within ourselves. This short meditation is one way to practice grounding; other options include the breathwork and physical movement suggestions in exercise 2 (page 57) and exercise 3 (page 59). You can also simply spend time outside to connect directly with the natural world, which in itself is very grounding. Coming back to this simple practice whenever you feel stressed, anxious, or scattered can help you begin to "rewire" your system to more readily tap into Self-energy. You can record the instructions and listen back if you would find that helpful.

Instructions

1. Settle yourself into a quiet, comfortable place, either standing or sitting with your feet on the floor (or if outside, on the ground), and take two or three deep breaths.

2. Softly close your eyes or soften your gaze and gently focus on the soles of your feet, noticing how they feel making contact with the surface below them.

3. Now imagine that within the arch of each foot is a small circular opening, like the shutter on a camera. Envision this shutter closing and reopening.

4. Keeping that shutter open in your mind's eye, notice what you feel through each foot as you allow the energy of the earth to draw up through each opening: Does it feel tingly or pulsing or so subtle that it's hard to detect? What happens to the energy as you picture it moving up both feet, into your legs, belly, torso, and lungs, and up into your head?

5. Take a few more breaths as you notice the earth's energy present in your body. Spend a few moments noticing any physical or emotional reactions, words, or images.

6. Let go of the shutter image and now imagine roots extending down through each foot deep into the earth. See if you can sense the anchoring energy of these roots spreading wide and deep.

7. As you breathe, exhale any tension, anxiety, or static energy down through the floor or ground and into the earth.

8. On your next inhale, draw up the earth's life force and nurturance through the "roots" of both feet, feeling that energy spreading throughout your body.

9. Continue to breathe and notice the sensations of energy in your body, and if it feels right to you, offer some sense of gratitude back to the earth for its support and presence.

10. Now, take a few more minutes to draw or express whatever came up for you. Maybe even write a reminder to yourself that you can repeat this exercise several times a day or anytime during your practice of IFS as needed.

Calming Breathwork Practices

What You'll Need

- 20 to 40 minutes of uninterrupted time
- A journal and pen, or digital notepad

Overview

Our breath is one of the most powerful tools available to us for calming our systems. It directly engages the parasympathetic nervous system (via the vagus nerve) to promote relaxation. Practicing deep breathing can improve mood, heart health, digestion, sleep, and pain management, and enhance mental focus and clarity. You can use these basic breathing exercises to send physiological signals of safety to your parts as you prepare to interact with them. As longtime IFS senior trainer Susan McConnell writes in *Somatic Internal Family Systems Therapy*, "When emotions begin to flood the system, the rhythmic waves of the breath can be an anchor in stormy emotional seas." This is an important reminder to return to the breath whenever you need to "reset" your system during activating work or as a helpful daily self-care practice.

Instructions

Practice A: Diaphragmatic "Belly" Breathing

This exercise involves using the abdominal muscles to fully engage the respiratory system. It can be done anywhere, at any time.

1. Settle into a comfortable position, either sitting up tall or lying down. Place one hand on your stomach and the other on your chest.

2. Take a deep breath in through your nose, gently and slowly, allowing your belly to expand like a balloon. Hold the breath there for a few moments.

3. Very slowly exhale through your nose, feeling your abdomen deflate as you breathe out all the air.

4. Repeat several more times and notice any changes in the sensations in your body or your emotions.

5. If you'd like, take a few minutes to note your experience in your journal.

Practice B: 4-7-8 Breathing

This technique involves breathing in intervals. It is widely used to relieve stress and anxiety, and can promote sleep.

1. Settle into a comfortable position, either sitting up tall or lying down.

2. Inhale gently through the nose as you slowly count to four.

3. Hold the breath for a count of seven (or as close to that as you can).

4. Exhale slowly through your nose as you count to eight.

5. Repeat for as long as it feels good to you.

6. If you'd like, take a few minutes to note your experience in your journal.

> TIP: If focusing on the breath counting in this particular way causes you to feel more stressed, just see if you can increase the length of your exhales, and think of smoothing out the breath as it moves in and out.

Movement for Settling the Nervous System

What You'll Need

- 20 to 45 minutes of uninterrupted time
- Yoga mat, floor, or bed
- Blankets and cushions (if needed)
- A journal and pen, or digital notepad

Overview

Combining breathwork with specific movement and body positioning stimulates the vagus nerve to send signals of physical and emotional safety, building stress resilience over time. Simple, gentle stretching combined with slow, intentional breathing has the potential to strengthen and recharge the nervous system effectively and fairly quickly. This helps us become active participants in our healing because of the powerful effect nervous system regulation has on releasing tension. It also paves the way for our Self-energy to be embodied as we physically *feel* the qualities of connectedness, clarity, calmness, and self-compassion. To further tone the vagus nerve while practicing these movements, hum, chant, or use the "ocean-sounding breath." To do this, inhale and then slightly constrict the back of your throat so that when you exhale, you make a sound like an ocean wave. It can take some practice, but once you get the sound going, you can use it for both the inhale and the exhale, allowing the exhale to be a little longer.

Practice A: Child's Pose

This is a deeply nurturing and tension-relieving position that also calms the mind.

1. Begin by kneeling, and sit back onto your heels, either keeping the knees together or separating them about as wide as your hips.

2. Exhale and fold forward, bringing your forehead to the floor or supporting it with a blanket or cushion. Either lay your hands alongside your torso, palms up, or stretch them out in front of you.

3. Relax the body, release through the shoulders, and focus on slow, steady ocean-sounding breaths or humming with each exhale; sink a bit deeper into the pose with your breath.

4. Stay here for at least a minute, about eight to ten slow breaths, and work up to about three to five minutes if you can. (If you have difficulty in this pose, place a folded blanket up between the backs of your legs and your ankles.)

5. To come up, slowly roll through your spine, vertebra by vertebra, with your head being the last to rise. Allow yourself to sit and breathe normally for a few moments.

6. If it's helpful, write down any sensations or feelings that may have come up for you, as this pose can sometimes facilitate emotional release.

Practice B: Legs Up the Wall

This is another deeply restorative pose that activates the parasympathetic nervous system and helps with anxiety, exhaustion, and weakened immunity (among its many benefits!).

1. Place your mat or blanket up against a clear wall with space enough to stretch your legs up along it.

2. Sit on your bottom with the right side of your body pushed against the wall. If it's more comfortable for you, sit on a cushion or folded blanket to raise your hips a bit.

3. Swivel your legs up onto the wall as you bring your back to the floor, keeping your bottom close to the wall. You can also use a cushion or folded blanket under your head and neck if that brings greater comfort.

4. Stay here for three to ten minutes, or whatever feels right to your body. Engage your ocean-sounding breath as you breathe in for four counts and out for eight counts (or just breathe normally if that feels better to you).

5. When you're ready, slide your legs back down to one side and sit up slowly and gently, allowing your normal breathing pattern to return.

6. If you'd like, write about what you noticed while in this pose.

Practice C: Vagus Nerve Reset for Nervous System Healing

This exercise is a way to relieve stress, anxiety, and trauma responses stored in the body. It is adapted from a YouTube video by Sukie Baxter, founder of Whole Body Revolution, which she credits learning from Stanley Rosenberg's book *Accessing the Healing Power of the Vagus Nerve*.

1. Begin by sitting up tall on your mat or blanket, and just turn your head from side to side, noticing any differences in the range of motion on each side as you do.

2. Lie down with your feet on the floor and knees bent, and interlace your fingers together, bringing your hands behind your head so that it is cradled in your hands. Your fingers should be just beneath the curve of your skull and just above where the head connects to the neck.

3. Using your hands to support your head so that you don't turn it, move just your eyes up and to the right and try to keep them there for about 30 seconds, breathing steadily. (You may need to work up to holding this position for that long. You may also notice that you feel the need to swallow or sigh or that your breath naturally deepens. These are all indications of positive vagus nerve shifts, which can occur as it is stimulated.)

4. Bring your eyes back to center and slowly sit up.

5. Once again sitting up tall, move your head from side to side and notice if it feels any different now, if your breathing is any easier, or if your range of motion is improved.

TIP: These are simple but powerful exercises that might produce tears or other physical forms of release. You may need to practice them in smaller increments depending on what is right for your body.

Body Awareness Scan

What You'll Need

- 20 to 60 minutes of uninterrupted time
- A journal, sketchpad, or digital notebook
- Pen, colored pencils, or markers (if desired)
- A recording device (if desired)

Overview

Bringing our awareness to sensations that arise in the body is an invaluable tool when beginning any IFS journey. Since our parts often use the body to express their needs or concerns, developing this practice as a way to compassionately tune into our inner world is one of the first steps on that path. Interestingly, doing a body scan is another way to stimulate the vagus nerve to promote relaxation and release tension. In this exercise, you'll be guided to notice emotional responses that you may also experience, as these can often indicate the presence of your parts. Taking your time with this exercise, if you can, will benefit your IFS work in the chapters to come. Be sure to completely read through all the steps or record the instructions and play them back so that your attention can remain in the body as much as possible as you do this.

Note: If working with your body in this way doesn't feel safe to you, it is important to respect this inner knowing and either skip this exercise or only do the parts you feel comfortable with.

Instructions

Part A: The Body Scan

1. Lie on the bed or the floor (using a yoga mat or blanket if needed) or sit up tall. Settle in so that you can be as comfortable as possible.

2. Take a few deep breaths and bring your attention to the body. Close your eyes or soften your gaze. Notice the rise and fall of the belly as you breathe, noting any particular sensations that are present now.

3. Starting at the top of your head, bring your awareness to any points of tension, discomfort, or pleasurable sensations that arise as you scan through the forehead, back of the head and neck, the throat and jaw, and the shoulders.

4. Extend your breath to any areas that feel tight or may be holding stress. Notice if there is a softening or release as you are present with these areas without an expectation that they do anything differently; let them know you are aware of them.

5. Continue scanning through the upper back and chest, the forearms, hands and fingers, the lower back, belly, and throughout the trunk of the body.

6. Notice if there is discomfort or a sense of "holding" in the abdomen, upper or lower back, and if there is, send some calming breaths to those areas.

7. Move your awareness to the waist, hips, groin, and buttocks, again scanning for tightness or anything that seems to want your attention and breathing compassion into those places.

8. Continue down through the thighs, calves, ankles, and feet, even wiggling the toes if that feels good.

9. Notice any additional points of tension. Again, send some calming breath into those areas.

10. When your scan feels complete, take another deep, full breath, and offer gratitude to the body for its messages and whatever you experienced.

Part B: Body Scan Map

1. Take a moment to notice any feelings or other sensations that might be present now, and note them in your journal.

2. Draw an outline of your body in whatever way feels right to you (it could even be a gingerbread-person shape), and color or highlight areas on the outline where you were aware of particular sensations or feelings.

3. Add whatever feeling words or descriptors to your highlighted areas that intuitively seem important. Draw any images that may have emerged onto your map in the areas of the body where this occurred, or use colors or even scribbles to represent what you felt in some way.

4. Now, as you look at your body scan map, what emotions or sensations are present?

5. Write about your experience in your journal: Take note of any reactions that occurred inside when you sent awareness to tense or constricted areas.

6. Reflect on how you are feeling toward your body and all that it holds for you.

7. Close with a note of gratitude for any parts that were physically present with you in this experience.

EXERCISE 5
Awareness of a Part

What You'll Need

- 20 to 60 minutes of uninterrupted time
- A journal, sketchpad, or digital notepad
- Pen, colored pencils, or markers (if desired)

Overview

To begin working with our parts, we need to first identify and invite them to know us when we are in Self—the state when we feel some of the 8 Cs (curious, compassionate, confident, clear, courageous, creative, calm, and connected). This relatively simple yet powerful practice can be done daily, or whenever possible, as it allows our parts to develop trust in us, the Self, so that they might then be more able and willing to reveal their stories, fears, and purpose to us within our internal system. If this feels difficult or too much for you at first, try to be gentle with yourself and take it slowly. Do your best to not feel urgency to come up with "the answers," but just give yourself time to see what comes. The most important thing here is to spend this time just noticing whatever is present inside.

Instructions

1. Settle into a comfortable position, either sitting or lying down, and take a couple of deep breaths.

2. Focus your attention inside: What physical sensations, points of tension, thoughts, or feelings are present?

3. Consider which of these you are most drawn toward and *how* you are experiencing it: Is it something you're mostly *hearing*, or do you *feel* it physically in a particular way? Do you *see* anything connected to or representing it?

4. Now check to see how you feel *toward* it. If the answer is *not* something like "open," "curious," "concerned," or "interested" (which it usually won't be initially), ask to hear more from whichever part is reacting. (Some common responses might be "I don't like it," or "I wish it would go away," or "It frustrates me.")

5. Ask if there is anything the reactive part wants you to know. Acknowledge and validate its concerns and respectfully request that it either step back, off to the side, or to just relax a bit once you have done so.

6. If a part has difficulty stepping back, spend some more time validating its concerns before respectfully repeating your request for it to relax. Offer your appreciation for its willingness to do that.

7. Ask yourself again how you feel toward the first part: Are you more open, curious, or compassionate now? Let it know this, and explore with it what it would like you to know and what it needs.

8. Allow the part to express itself as fully as it can: Invite it to show you how it would like to be represented in your journal. Draw and write what it tells you about itself, if it does.

9. Ask the part if it would like you to come back to spend more time with it later. If so, make a plan with it to do so.

10. Extend your gratitude to this part and for all it just shared with you. If it feels right, you could offer a physical gesture that feels soothing and kind to your system, such as placing a hand on your chest or wherever you physically felt this part's energy.

TIP: Some people have difficulty becoming aware of a part. See "I Don't Feel Anything" on page 79 for an example of how to work with that.

Part Two

STEP-BY-STEP SELF-LED IFS

No one you have been . . . ever leaves you. The new parts of you simply jump in the car and go along for the rest of the ride. The success of your journey and your destination all depend on who's driving.

—Bruce Springsteen, singer-songwriter
and musician, from *Born to Run*

This part will lead you through the basics of practicing IFS on your own by first focusing on each step on this path and offering exercises designed to help you better understand and explore your inner world from a place of curiosity and compassion. We'll delve further into the nature and functions of our manager and firefighter parts as well. Then, we'll close by taking a look at particular challenges that may emerge along the way with specific strategies for handling them.

It is vitally important to continue to hone your skills of listening inside for direction as you progress through this part. I encourage you to return to particular exercises or chapters you've already found helpful to remain grounded and well supported both physically and emotionally. Also, taking breaks from the work, especially if you find that something is particularly intense for your internal family system, may also be a good idea. The great thing is that your parts are always with you and will still be there when you're ready to return!

CHAPTER THREE

Meeting Your Parts for the First Time

As you set off on your Self-led IFS path, this chapter provides you with a detailed trail map. You will begin by charting your way through a low-stakes experience of encountering and learning to acknowledge, appreciate, and start to understand one or more of your parts as a first step.

Before You Begin

Intentionally setting the stage for your first IFS session is a genuine way of letting your internal family system know at the outset that you, the Self, can be relied upon to attend to its needs. As I've mentioned, the most important issue for our parts is *safety*, and it is likely that you already intuitively know what's necessary for you to feel a sense of safety to begin this work. For some people, it may be important to have a block of time available when no one else is present to avoid interruptions and distractions. For others, it may feel more settling to have the supportive energy of other people or pets around to help them feel more grounded.

You can try different options to determine what feels right for *your* system, keeping in mind that what is most important is to find a quiet, safe, and comfortable place that is sustainable and relaxing for you. Ideally, this should be a setting where disturbances are unlikely, freeing up your attention to focus internally for an hour or more. This may mean that you'll have to let others know that you'll need this uninterrupted time and space. Also, try to minimize other distractions, such as notifications from your phone or computer. You want to send a clear message to your parts that they are your top priority during this time, so be sure to take whatever steps are necessary to reinforce this.

Allowing yourself plenty of time to let your IFS exploration unfold is also a consideration, as it is helpful for your system to not feel pressured. Setting aside at least an hour or more this first time is wise to provide ample opportunity to center yourself, then engage with your parts as fully as possible, and finish by processing the experience. Another reason ample time is necessary, especially as you begin, is that to feel safe, our parts need to sense that there is no agenda to get somewhere in particular or to effect change. Giving our parts with such concerns plenty of reassurance that this isn't the case allows for a more trusting relationship with you, the Self, to develop.

It is key to remember that you are entering your internal family system with an *offering*—not any sort of directive—to deepen your connection with your parts. This is why it's so important to keep in mind that, as you do begin to find and work with your parts, you check back in with them periodically to remain connected and build trust overall in your system. Making a gentle commitment to return to your parts to see how they are doing in the week or so following your initial work with them helps them to know that you are a reliable and consistent presence.

Step One: FIND My Part(s)

This first step is all about turning your attention inward and tuning into whatever bodily sensations, thoughts, images, or emotional feelings might be present. This helps you learn what part or parts might need your attention in the present moment. Taking your time to feel your way into this is a good idea, especially if the notion of "going inside" is new to you. Allowing yourself to just *notice* and not evaluate, figure out, or do anything about what is present internally may take a bit of practice. See if you can stay with it as this is the way your parts can make themselves known to you.

Instructions

1. Find a comfortable position either sitting up or lying down. Take two or three slow, deep breaths, letting both feet be grounded on the floor or just noticing your body's points of contact with whatever is supporting you (e.g., chair, floor, or bed).

2. If it's helpful, close your eyes or soften your gaze. Keeping your eyes open is also fine. Do whatever feels right to you to shift your focus inward.

3. *Notice* whatever physical sensations, points of tension, thoughts, feelings, or images might be present.

4. Continue to sit quietly, breathe, and notice what else wants to emerge, or if anything shifts inside as you do this.

TIP: If this step is difficult for you, refer back to the "Body Awareness Scan" on page 63. Review your journal entries on the body scan. Two other helpful exercises for this step (including your journal responses to them) are "Getting Grounded" on page 55 and "Awareness of a Part" on page 66.

Step Two: FOCUS on and FLESH OUT a Target Part

These two steps are often combined and are about recognizing and coming to understand your "target" part a bit better. As you concentrate on whatever has arisen inside, give it time and space to let you know whether it would like your attention now and provide you with more information about itself so that you can begin to have a clearer sense of who it is. This helps acknowledge that the part is present and lets it know that you are attending to it by listening closely to what it wants you to know about itself and asking it to show itself to you more completely.

Instructions

1. As you sit quietly and breathe, focus on whatever thought, sensation, or feeling you have become aware of that seems to want to be the focus of your attention in this moment.

2. Acknowledge its presence by sending it some appreciation for coming forward and reassure it that it now has your attention.

3. Ask it to show or tell you more about itself, what it needs, what it's being activated by, or whatever it would like you to know about itself.

4. Briefly thank it for communicating whatever it has to you.

> TIP: For help with this step, check out "Getting to Know Your Parts" on page 83 and refer back to "Awareness of a Part" on page 66.

Step Three: How Do You FEEL TOWARD This Part?

This is the inquiry that is used in IFS work to determine the degree to which Self-energy is present in relation to a part. Very often another part (or parts) is blended with Self, and this blended part will react to the target part—the part you're currently trying to get to know. You'll recognize this is happening because there will be feelings that are NOT like the 8 Cs; these feelings come from the blended part (or several parts) that are reacting to the target part. When this happens, acknowledge their presence, listen to their concerns, and respectfully request that they step back. Then again, ask yourself, "How do I feel toward this part now?" to continue to unblend until the answer you come to indicates that what is left is Self (which you'll recognize when you feel some of the 8 Cs; see page 19). It is essential to spend whatever time you need for this step to begin establishing a true "Self-to-part" relationship.

Instructions

1. As you continue to be present with the part that has emerged as the focus of your session, ask yourself, "How do I *feel* toward this part?"

2. Allow some time for the answer to arise naturally within you, rather than rushing to figure out the "right" answer (that urge indicates that another part is reacting). This can take a little practice, but be as patient as possible to facilitate the discovery of more parts and the uncovering of more Self-energy, which is necessary for the work to go well.

3. If the answer you receive is anything other than curious, open, concerned, neutral, calm, connected, or any of the other 8 Cs (and this is generally often the case), then you know another part is present and is reacting to the target part receiving your attention.

4. Ask the reacting part to tell you a bit more about how it is feeling and validate its response. When it feels like the reactive part has been acknowledged and feels heard, ask it respectfully to step back or off to the side to allow you to continue getting to know the target part. Reassure it that you don't want it to go away completely, but that it would be most helpful if it didn't interrupt, if that would be possible, and be sure to thank it for doing so.

5. Return to the target part, and ask yourself again, "How do I feel toward this part now?" Repeat steps two to four until your response is something like curious, open, calm, interested, or even OK.

6. Once all of your parts have unblended from Self and you are present in Self-energy, let the target part know how *you* feel toward it now, and give it some time to fully take that in.

7. If any of the other parts that did react to this inquiry did not feel comfortable relaxing or stepping back, let the target part know that you will come back to it and allow the reactive one to now become the target part.

TIP: If you need additional ideas or help with this step, go back to "Awareness of a Part" on page 66 and check out "Getting to Know Your Parts" on page 83 and "Blending and Unblending" on page 85.

Step Four: BEFRIEND the Target Part

Now that some separation has been created between you (the Self) and the part you've chosen to focus on, the *relationship* between you and this part is formed and becomes the focus. Because IFS is a relational model, inviting active communication with your target part in this step helps create the connection needed to promote trust and healing. Establishing trust between parts and Self is the cornerstone of your work with them. Once they feel more trusting of Self, your work with your parts can deepen and will likely progress much more smoothly.

Instructions

1. Now that you are present with your target part with Self-energy on board, again let it know of your curiosity about it or compassion for it, and gently ask it how it responds to that.

2. Ask this part what it is trying to accomplish for you or what it feels its job is, how it came to be in this role and how long it has been doing it, and how it is trying to help your system overall.

3. If it feels important, you can also ask it what its relationship with the other parts that may have reacted to it earlier is like, or if there is anything else it would like you to know about its story.

4. Respond by letting it know how valuable it is, validate how hard it is working on your behalf, and acknowledge your respect for its efforts in keeping your internal system safe. You can reinforce this with soothing physical gestures if that feels right to you.

5. If you find it helpful, jot down this part's responses in your journal.

TIP: "Dialoguing with Parts" on page 87 is a helpful way to communicate with and establish ongoing dialogues with your parts. "Getting to Know Your Parts" on page 83 may also give you additional ideas for this step.

Step Five: Ask the Target Part about Its FEARS

This is a very important step because it generally provides a lot of information about what is keeping this part in its role. You may come to understand more about this part's relationships with other protectors here, especially those the target part may be in conflict with. The most likely response to this inquiry about the part's fears, however, will have something to do with the exile it protects, so expressing your deep respect and understanding around this aspect of its functioning serves to strengthen the developing trust between Self and this part even more.

Instructions

1. As you are acknowledging your target part's efforts in its mission to keep you safe, ask it what it thinks would happen if it wasn't doing this job, if it took a break from doing it, or even just relaxed a little bit.

2. Once it responds to this question (or questions), follow up by respectfully asking what it thinks would be so bad about that happening and why it feels that way.

3. Validate the feelings it expresses around its fears, and gently ask what, if anything, it thinks might be helpful to it in this regard.

4. Now check with this part to determine if it would like to continue talking with you now or at a later time, and reassure it that either option works for you. If you actually don't have much time left in your session, just let the part know that and make a plan with it to check in at a later time.

> TIP: "Dialoguing with Parts" on page 87 can help you with this step.

Step Six: Say Goodbye and Conclude the Session

As you come to the end of your Self-led IFS session, it is extremely important to offer additional validation and gratitude to the part that had the courage to step forward to begin this journey with you.

Instructions

1. Thank this part for its honesty and willingness to share all that it was able to in this session. Ask it if there is anything else it needs before the session concludes. If it feels right, you can reinforce your deep appreciation for your part's hard work with physical gestures of self-compassion, too, such as placing a hand on your chest or wherever you felt the energy of that part.

2. Extend some gratitude to the parts that graciously stepped back so that you could complete this work with your target part, reassuring them that they will have an opportunity, as well, to talk with you at another time.

3. Ask your target part if it would like you to check back in with it at some point soon to see how it's doing. See if it can be specific about this so that you can be sure to follow through with your commitment to do this.

4. Conclude with two or three breaths to let your system know that the session is ending. Offer some additional appreciation to all of your parts (and yourself!) for giving you permission to turn inward to explore their world a bit during this time.

Self-Led Session: "I Don't Feel Anything"

Many people who try IFS for the first time have difficulty noticing their parts at first. It's quite common for certain parts to try to block our awareness of other parts in the system in order to do their jobs. So, even when it seems as though there aren't any parts present, it is still possible for us to get some sense of our parts. This session illustrates that experience.

To begin, I take a couple of deep breaths, settle into a comfortable space, and close my eyes to tune into what I am feeling in my body:

Right away I notice a slight numbness around my chest and a sense of blankness in my head; as I send some breath to those areas, nothing changes . . .

I decide to explore whether or not the numbness and blankness might be parts trying to either get my attention or working to block other parts from coming into my awareness, so I continue to focus on these sensations . . .

TANIS (T): "I'm noticing you, Numbness and Blankness, and I am wondering if there is any way you could help me understand more about you right now? Maybe there is a word or something you could show me? I do appreciate that you're here, and I have a feeling that you must have a very good reason for showing up in this way."

I continue to just breathe for a few minutes, and eventually the blank feeling in my head seems to intensify a bit.

T: "Well, I'm continuing to notice you there in my head, Blankness, and I am sensing you getting a bit stronger right now. Might it be possible for you to give me just one word or show me more to help me understand you better?"

The blank feeling in my head remains the same, so I just wait and continue to breathe and send some calming energy to it. After another few minutes, I see an image of a blank wall.

T: "I so appreciate that you're sending me this image now . . ."

(I check inside to see how I feel toward this part that seems to be showing up as a blank wall. I notice some frustration and confusion toward it.)

T: "OK, I totally get that you, Frustration and Confusion, are reacting the way that you are. Anything else you need me to know?"

FRUSTRATION AND CONFUSION (FC): "This is aggravating and doesn't make any sense."

T: "I understand your concerns completely. Would it be OK with the two of you if I continue to just be with this part to see if there may be more it wants to show? If it can, things might become more clear and less frustrating right now."

FC: "OK, but we're not really sure that will help."

T: "I get that, but if you could step back just a little, and try not to interrupt us so that I can check it out, that would be great. I really appreciate you two sharing what

you have with me right now, and I know you're trying to help . . ."

They do step back, and I offer them thanks for this as well.

I notice that the blank wall is still there, and I check to see how I feel toward it. I find that I now feel a little curious about it, so I decide to let it know this.

T: "I am still noticing you there, Blankness, and just want you to know that now I do feel curious toward you. Is there anything more you could let me know about you?"

BLANKNESS (B): "I don't know . . ."

T: "OK, I really appreciate you being able to tell me that. Anything else about that or what you're trying to do for me right now?"

Again, I see the blank wall, but now I get a strong sense of a "blocking" energy with it.

T: "I'm getting the sense from what you're showing me and having me feel has to do with you blocking something, is that right?"

B: "Yes."

T: "Can you tell or show me more?"

B: "No."

Suddenly I hear a different voice that says, "This will get you nowhere."

T: "Oh, OK. Are you another part?"

NEW PART (N): "Uh-huh, and I'm saying this will get you nowhere."

I mostly experience this new part as a voice in my head, so I check to see how I feel toward it, and I find that I still feel pretty curious . . .

T: "OK, would you be willing to help me understand better who you are?"

N: "No, I'm not going to let you do this because it doesn't make any sense."

T: "Well, I can certainly understand that you might be skeptical. Can you tell me more about what you're trying to do for me right now?"

SKEPTICAL PART (S): "It seems to me that you're just making all this up in your head, and I think it's going to backfire."

T: "OK, so it sounds like you're trying to protect me from things

backfiring and going badly, is that right?"

S: "Absolutely. I just don't think doing this makes any logical sense."

T: "I totally get that you feel that way, and I can really feel how hard you're working right now to take care of me. How long have you been doing this for me, in this way?"

S: "Since you were a kid. You just haven't been paying that much attention . . ."

T: "Yes, that's true, but I am here now, and I'm really glad that you can let me know all this. That seems like a long time that you've been taking care of me this way . . . what do you think might happen to me if you ever took a break from this work that you're doing for me?"

S: "I think you'd just get into a big mess that you probably couldn't get out of—like with the IFS stuff you're trying to do now."

T: "Well, it makes a lot of sense to me that you have to make sure that doesn't happen. Has that happened in the past, that I've gotten into a big mess when I tried something new?"

S: "Of course it has, so I have to keep doing this to make sure that it doesn't happen again. I just think you will get overwhelmed and that would be really bad."

T: "I understand, and it's very clear to me that you want to protect me from all that. But I feel pretty strongly that we can really be OK doing this IFS stuff, especially if we go really slowly. I feel like it could help us a lot, but I also want to make sure that it's OK with you."

S: "I'm not really convinced, but I do feel like you're beginning to understand where I'm coming from. I felt like I just had to send Blankness in so that you really couldn't do anything and possibly get yourself hurt."

T: "That makes a lot of sense, and I so appreciate you telling me that. Would you be willing to continue to talk about this together? It feels very important to me, and I want to understand more about how you and Blankness work together."

S: "Yeah, I guess that would be all right . . ."

T: "Thank you so much—would it be OK if I check back in with you in the next few days?"

S: "Yes, that would be good . . . you still have a lot to learn."

T: "I totally agree, and am so grateful that both you and Blankness could be with me today . . . this has been very eye-opening for me."

Getting to Know Your Parts

What You'll Need

- 20 to 45 minutes of uninterrupted time
- A journal, sketchpad, or digital notebook
- Pen, colored pencils, or markers (if desired)

Overview

Adapted with permission from *Parts Work* by long-time IFS therapist and educator Tom Holmes, PhD, this exercise is intended to help you broaden your awareness of your parts as you might come to notice them going about your daily activities. You may not feel as though you can answer all these questions directly yet, since you are just beginning your IFS journey, but see if you can allow yourself to go with your intuition here and play with the questions a bit. You can come back to this exercise again and again as you gain clarity around getting to know your parts.

Instructions

1. Situate yourself comfortably and take a few deep breaths. Bring to mind a situation or set of circumstances in your life now or in the past that creates a strong reaction in you.

2. Write whatever comes to you as you consider the following questions about your reaction:

   - What feelings are connected to this reaction?
   - *How* do you notice the reactions or those feelings in your body?
   - Where in your body do you feel them? Jot down or draw this in your journal—it could be words, colors, scribbles, or an image of that area of your body with the feeling in it.

- Are any thoughts present that seem to go with that reaction? If so, write them out.
- Do you have a sense of what this part or parts would like to say? If you do, write as much of what this part(s) needs to express as you can.
- If you can, allow an image to come to mind to represent this part. Can you envision what it might look like? If so, draw it or write about how it looks to you.

3. Consider how you might notice parts as you go through your day. Jot down your responses to the following:

- Are there particular situations that could activate any parts for you? If so, what might those be?
- What feelings and actions might accompany the reactions of these parts?
- Do you have a sense of the roles these parts play?
- Can you tell how they try to help you?
- Do you notice how those around you react when that part or parts is around?
- What comes up for you after that part(s) has been present?
- Do you notice any reactivity inside toward the part that has been present (in the form of thoughts, strong emotions, or physical sensations), possibly from other parts that might frequently react to it in this way?

4. Thinking of your parts as your helpers, see if you can notice and make a list of the following parts that might be present in your internal family system:

- Parts that help you get things done.
- Parts that help you know and assert your needs.
- Parts that help you play, relax, and have fun.

5. Draw or brainstorm about these parts in whatever way is helpful as you conclude.

Blending and Unblending

What You'll Need

- 20 to 40 minutes of uninterrupted time
- A journal, sketchpad, or digital notebook
- Pen, colored pencils, or markers (if desired)

Overview

To notice, better understand, and effectively work with your parts, some degree of "unblending" needs to occur. What can be tricky for our parts, though, is that blending with us is generally how they do their jobs. Often this has been happening for years without our awareness. Our parts naturally blend with us to help us manage our lives in various ways and to help us relax when we need to, among so many other functions. So, while blending is not a bad thing and can happen fluidly and harmoniously in *connection* with Self-energy, the difficulty comes when this process becomes more extreme—that is, when the parts don't yet trust or know the Self and feel they must take over to ensure the system's safety. This exercise is intended to help you discern the "felt sense" of being blended with or "in" a part versus the awareness of being unblended from or "with" a part.

Instructions

1. Situate yourself comfortably, and take a few deep breaths. Bring back to mind a part you have explored that has a strong reaction to a situation or even a particular person in your life. (This may be one from the previous exercise or another that comes through to you right now.)

2. If you developed an image of this part, bring this to mind as well. If not, see if you can hear what it typically says to you or how you notice it in your body.

3. Now, instead of trying to separate from this part, allow yourself to embody it more fully in some way. This could be playing out the behaviors that it typically does or saying the words out loud that you normally hear it saying.

4. Notice in your body how it feels to "be" this part for a few minutes. Jot down some notes about this in your journal if you'd like.

5. Thank this part for more fully coming into your body (if it did) and see if you can tell now how *you* feel toward it.

6. It makes complete sense if you notice other parts reacting to this one. Let them know that they can tell you whatever they need you to know right now.

7. Once this feels complete with the reactive parts, check again how you feel toward the first part. When you notice some openness, curiosity, compassion, etc., let it know that, and just see if it responds in any way.

8. Ask this part, if you can, how it feels to it to be fully blended with you when it does what it does for you. Note whatever it says in your journal.

9. Ask this part what it feels like for you to be more present with it. Note its response.

10. Offer some gratitude to this part for allowing you to "play" with it a bit during this time, and let it know that you'd like to continue getting to know it if that would be all right with it.

11. Write or draw anything that feels important to either you or this part as you conclude.

Dialoguing with Parts

What You'll Need

- 30 to 60 minutes (or more) of un-interrupted time
- A journal, sketchpad, or digital notepad
- Pen, colored pencils, or markers (if desired)

Overview

Often in our IFS work our parts need us to hear them fully and completely, which helps them feel validated and "seen." This also helps us to continue to build a trusting relationship with them, as well as to gain a deeper understanding of their role, their desires, and their needs. This exercise is a way to somewhat externalize your conversations with your parts. It is a good tool for noticing shifts in their narratives over time as well. This is something you can do whenever it feels necessary to capture everything a part would like you to know. It also affords you the opportunity to respond to the part in a concrete way (which our parts usually need and really appreciate!).

Instructions

1. Settle into a comfortable position and take a few deep breaths.

2. Ask if there are any parts that need your attention. If one comes forward, note how you feel toward it, unblending from any other parts that may be reacting to it until you can be present with it in Self (revisit the previous exercise if you need help with this).

3. If you don't have a part stepping forward, ask the reactive part that you worked with in the previous exercise if it would be open to doing this with you now, being sure that you are present with it in Self-energy.

4. Ask the part to write, sketch, or draw whatever it needs you to know about itself right now (e.g., its concerns, its story, etc.) in as complete a way as it can, using as many pages of your journal as needed. Let it know that anything it needs to express is important and valid to you.

5. Once the part feels that it has communicated everything it can, use a page of your journal that faces the part's entry (if possible) to record your response to it.

6. Continue taking turns with your part as you both express and respond to each other in your journal until the experience feels complete for the time being.

7. Thank this part for having the courage to come forward in this way and for all that it expressed to you. Ask if it might like to continue doing this from time to time.

Mandala Mapping

What You'll Need

- 20 to 45 minutes of uninterrupted time
- Your journal, sketchpad, or digital notebook
- A pen, colored pencils, or markers (as desired)

Overview

As you learned on page 23, the IFS mandala was conceived and created by longtime IFS clinician and teacher Janet Mullen, LCSW. It has been used as a teaching tool and graphic illustration of our internal family systems now for decades. The word *mandala* actually means "circle," which is how many of us in the IFS community see our inner world of parts. It is also a symbol of wholeness, which makes it appropriate for our work here, showing us the interconnectedness of parts and Self. In this exercise, you will have the opportunity to fill in your own IFS mandala. As your journey progresses, you can come back to this exercise and work on it further.

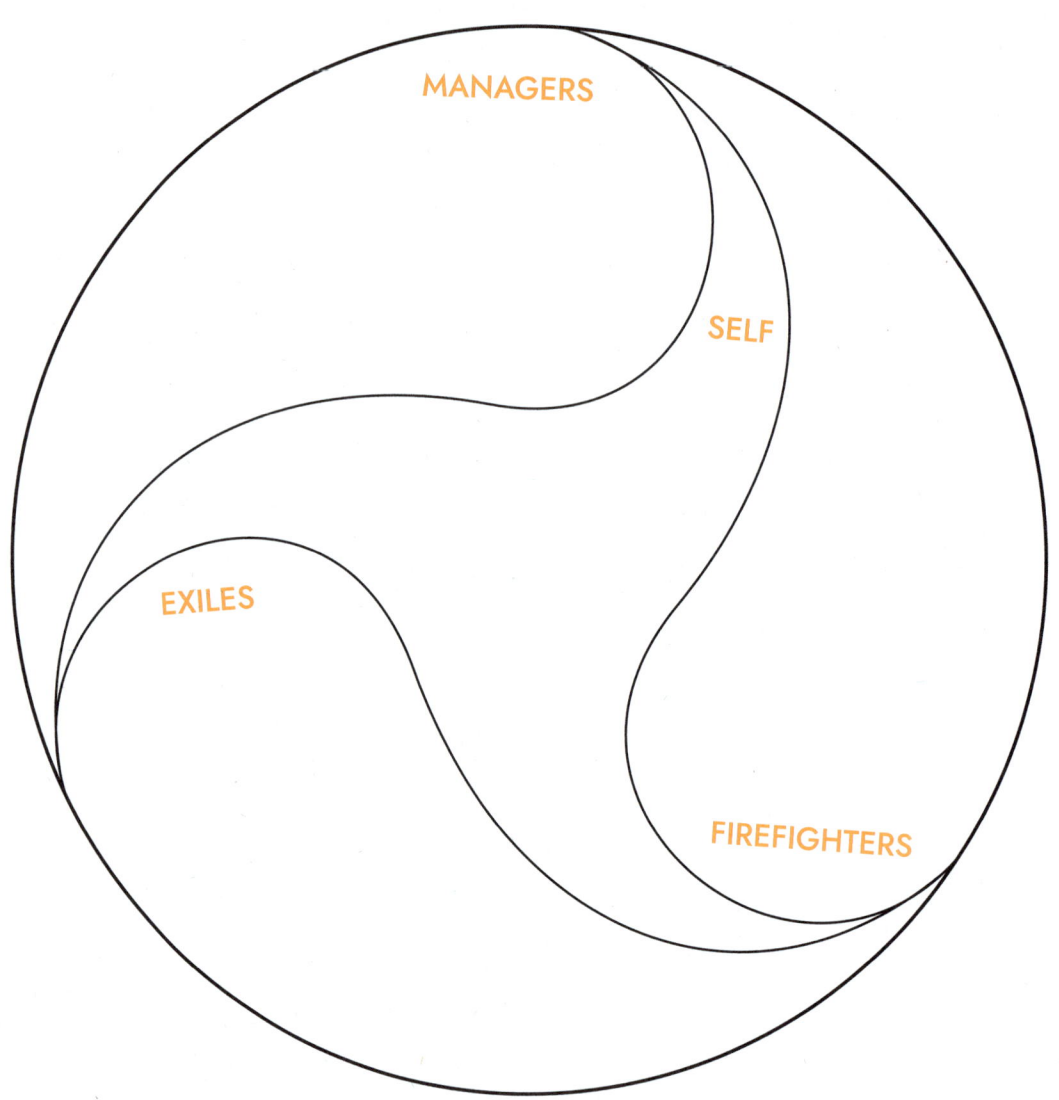

Instructions

1. Make yourself comfortable and take two or three deep breaths.

2. Go back to page 23 and reread the entries in the IFS mandala. Take note of any internal reactions. Notice if any of the examples of parts listed there resonate with you now.

3. Using the blank mandala, fill in the sections corresponding to the different categories of parts with parts of your own that you have already begun to know, or if that has not yet occurred, fill it in with what your intuition is telling you in terms of parts that are likely to be present in your system.

4. You can also use colors or images to illustrate parts in your mandala, or you can use additional words if that feels right for you.

5. Looking at how you've filled in your mandala, write about what you notice and whatever is coming up for you in your journal.

CHAPTER FOUR

Working with Your Manager Parts

You are now at the next step on your IFS journey toward deepening your relationship with the parts that make up your personal "protective system"—in this case, your managers. This chapter is a guided approach to better understanding and working with these valuable and motivated parts of us that work hard to stay on top of things in our everyday lives. They help us reach our goals, stay organized and "in control," maintain our relationships, and generally attempt to manage things so that perceived disaster is averted, internally and externally. Their tireless efforts to do what's "right" for us can be challenging to fully appreciate at times, so let's take a closer look at what our managers are all about and how you can start working with them.

Understanding Manager Parts

Our managers are typically the parts that we most easily notice, as they tend to be the ones that are present, active, and involved in our daily functioning. Common roles they have taken on include the people-pleaser, the skeptic or doubter, the inner critic, the self-sacrificing caretaker, the intellectual analyzer, the controlling taskmaster, the minimizer, the fixer or rescuer, the overly responsible helper, the anxious worrier, the overachiever, and even the highly driven "self-improver." This is by no means a complete list since our own group of managers is as unique as we are, given that it has developed as a result of our personal experiences in the particular family and culture we grew up in.

That said, certain types of manager parts do appear fairly frequently in many people's systems. These include various types of critics (the perfectionist, the judge, the taskmaster, etc.), thinking or "head" parts (such as the intellectual one, the skeptic, or planning and analyzing parts), and very often, worried or anxious parts. These parts have usually stepped into the positions they hold early in our lives. When asked how old they are, most will report being elementary school age or just a bit older. Because of this, they often think *we* are still young and don't have the resources to handle things without their help. In this sense, they are inner children who have had to grow up too fast, carrying their own burdens of responsibility and fear, though many of them want to appear strong and even "tough" in these roles in order to be effective. They generally don't see any other option beyond continuing to do what they've always done for us and are convinced they have no other choice.

Some of these parts also tend to feel extremely alone—especially our critics and other managers that are disliked, and even hated, by other parts in the system due to the nature of their jobs. Despite all this, they remain resolutely committed to their mission of proactive protection, both for the exile (or exiles) that they're attached to, as well as for the entire system. Such dedication results in our managers becoming stuck in these roles, even though they are overworked and exhausted by them; they truly believe that if they allow vulnerability to surface that our safety is at risk and we'll be hurt—again. So, they blend with us because they feel that they have to, often slipping into the driver's seat without our awareness.

Acknowledgment and appreciation for how hard they work top the list of things that our managers need to begin to heal. Because they often have little to no awareness that there *is* a Self that is both available to them and worthy of their trust, slowly building a relationship with them in which they can be fully known is key here. This involves becoming more able to *notice* their presence, and then beginning to comprehend the difficult systemic constraints that keep them bound to their roles. Respect, reassurance, and validation are foundational to this practice since our managers really need us to understand their functioning from the perspective of their true positive intention for us, not just in terms of what their role has become.

Tips for Working with Manager Parts

We need to remember that our managers have the need to *matter* and to *help* us as we continue to work with them. Bringing our awareness to them from a place of curiosity and compassion can be transformative in itself; they have been so used to operating only from their own limited perspective that bringing in Self's larger view along with a caring concern for them is often very healing. At times, and with certain parts, this can be challenging to do, however. This is why it is essential to continually work to *unblend* from other parts that react to managers like our harsh critics, passive-pessimists, highly anxious parts, or self-sacrificing caretakers.

We can only be fully present and communicate our respect to parts like these when we are firmly grounded in Self-energy. It is crucial to *listen* to and sincerely *value* both the contributions and concerns of our managers, as this is not something they are accustomed to experiencing. It can often help them to reveal the deeper aspects of who they are, what they need, and what they want for us. Truly honoring them and the vast amount of energy they expend on our behalf helps to develop deep and collaborative relationships with them.

Step One: Reconnect with My Manager Part(s)

This step involves inviting a part or parts that you may have encountered in chapter 3 to continue your work together. It's highly likely that the "target" part you met was one (or more) of your managers, and this is an opportunity to begin the process of learning more about them.

Instructions

1. Settle into a comfortable space, sitting up tall or lying down, and take in a few slow, deep breaths. Turn your awareness inward, closing your eyes or softening your gaze if that's helpful to you.

2. Tune into whatever sensations or points of tension are present in your body. As you do, send some breath to those places in your body, and gently ask if there is a part or parts that would like your attention now, or if the one you previously met would like to reconnect.

3. Notice if an image, voice, or heightened bodily sensation arises, and let it know you are present with it.

4. See if you can tell how you feel toward whatever shows up. If this isn't something like curious, open, compassionate, neutral,

caring, or interested, then check in with whatever other part or parts might be reacting to this one. Listen to and validate its concerns, and ask it if it will step back a bit and not interrupt while you work with the first part. Thank it for doing so.

5. Check again to determine how you feel toward your target part, and repeat the previous step until you are in Self and able to be present with it from a place of compassion, curiosity, kindness, concern, or openness.

6. Now, gently inquire about how this part has been doing since you met with it last time (if it is that part), and if there is anything else it would like you to know right now. If this part is not the same one that you met earlier, ask it to let you know more about itself in whatever way feels right.

7. Write down anything the part tells you in your journal if that feels helpful.

TIP: For assistance with this step, try out "Manager Meditation" on page 111 or go back to "Getting to Know Your Parts" on page 83.

Step Two: Deepen the Dialogue with This Manager Part

Once our managers sense that they have our undivided attention and that we will listen fully to them in all their complexity, their trust in us grows. Therefore, the intention of this step is to continue developing awareness and understanding of the manager you have just established contact with in the previous step.

Instructions

1. Continue the conversation you began with this manager in the previous step, asking any follow-up questions that come to you based on what it has been able to share with you so far.

2. Ask yourself again how you *feel toward* this part to check for the presence of other reactive parts and to determine the degree to which you are still in Self as you engage with this part.

3. If other parts are reacting, listen to and validate their concerns and respectfully ask that they step back so that you can continue working with this manager part. Thank them for doing so.

4. Gently ask this manager part to remind you what it feels its job is or what it is trying to accomplish for you. Once it lets you know this, follow up with any clarifying questions that feel necessary so that you can fully understand what it means. Reflect this back to it if that feels right.

5. Now ask this part if it can tell or show you about how old it is and at what point in your life it stepped into this role. Again, ask for clarification if needed.

6. Reassure your manager that it has all the time and space it needs to let you know these things—that it's not necessary for its responses to come quickly, or at all, and that you are just hoping to understand it more completely as you spend time with it here.

7. Check again with this part to see if there is more it would like to share regarding the concerns it has if it wasn't doing this job, or if it even relaxed a little in this role, again reflecting back to it what it tells you to make sure you understand fully.

8. Gently inquire if there is anything else this manager would like you to know about its story or what it tries to do to help the internal family system overall.

9. Extend your gratitude for all this part has been able to share with you in this step.

TIP: Try "My Manager's Story" on page 114 for additional support with this step.

Step Three: Establish a Two-Way Relationship with This Manager Part

When our parts come to know us more fully, they can begin to trust that *we* are safe and that we can be depended upon to help them now by being present and attending to them in whatever ways they may need. Therefore, the purpose of this step is to continue deepening your relationship with this part by checking in with it regarding its awareness of *you*, the Self.

Instructions

1. As your conversation continues to unfold with this manager, let it know that you're curious about how it feels toward *you*, and whether or not it can *feel* you there with it right now.

2. If it doesn't quite know yet how to respond to this, reassure it that it makes sense that it might need space to "feel out" this connection with you and that it will likely take some time for the relationship between you to develop, which is totally OK and understandable.

3. Depending on how it responds to you, you can also ask this part how old it thinks *you* are (which will likely be a much younger age than you actually are), and either tell it or show it the age you are now.

4. Discuss its reaction to this together, checking to see if there is more this part would like to know about you.

5. If it feels intuitively right, also ask this manager how it feels to it that you are present spending time with it now and if there is anything it needs or would like your support with.

> TIP: "My Manager's Story" on page 114 is intended to assist you further with this step.

Step Four: Gain a Deeper Understanding of This Manager's Role

The goal of this step is to expand your awareness of the role this manager plays in your internal family system overall. This includes the nature of its relationships with other parts and the constraints it may feel as a result of this.

Instructions

1. As you continue to sit with this manager part, ask it how it feels about its job. Does it *like* this role? Are there aspects of its job that are particularly difficult for it?

2. Encourage this part to express to you as much as it can about what might be hard for it within the system overall. Is there more it wants to say about this?

3. Inquire now about this manager's *relationships* with other parts. How does it feel toward or get along with the parts that may have been reactive to it at the beginning of this session (or when you first met it)? Can it tell you anything more about other parts with whom it may be particularly allied or in conflict with?

4. Offer reassurance to your manager, again, that your hope is to become increasingly *aware* of how all the parts inside are interrelated and work together. If it doesn't feel ready or able to discuss these things right now, assure it that you understand and are confident you will come to know this over time.

5. Now, ask your manager if it might be able to let you know anything about the part or parts that it protects. It may have alluded to this when asked earlier about its concerns regarding what might happen if it wasn't doing its job or even relaxed in its work a bit. Invite it here to clarify whether or not these concerns are connected to a specific vulnerable part that it protects, though it may or may not have full awareness of this (which is totally fine).

6. Extend your gratitude for all that this manager has been able to share with you in this step, and jot down what you've learned in your journal for later reference.

TIP: Helpful exercises for this step are "My Manager's Story" on page 114 and "Manager Mapping" on page 117.

Step Five: Invite Continued Collaboration and Conclude the Session with This Manager Part

The intention of this step is to integrate what you've learned from this part and to express your desire to continue a collaborative relationship with it. Because being with you in this way is initially an unfamiliar experience, it is powerful and necessary at this point to offer your continued presence and gratitude to this part (and the other parts that tend to react to it) for the commitment and courage it has shown while being with you during this session.

Instructions

1. If it feels helpful to review what this manager has expressed to you about its role, concerns, and its relationships with other parts in your internal system, do that now.

2. Reiterate your deep appreciation and respect for everything this part does for you and its position in your internal family, acknowledging the courage it took for it to engage with you more fully during this time.

3. Ask this part (along with the parts that stepped back so you could work with this one) whether it feels that this time together has been helpful to it and how it would like to stay connected with you.

4. Reflecting on some of the specific difficulties that this part has shared with you that it experiences in its role, inquire if it might like some assistance or support from you with those concerns and how it feels you could best help.

5. Invite this part (along with any others that stepped back initially) to let you know if it would like you to check in with it in a particular way moving forward (e.g., every day, at a particular time of

day, a couple of times a week, or whenever you notice it), and if it does, make a note of that.

6. Say goodbye for the time being and indicate your intention to follow through with staying connected to both this manager and the others you had contact with in this session in order to continue to strengthen your ongoing relationships with them.

> TIP: For further support and reflection in this step, check out "Manager Mapping" on page 117.

The relationship your parts have with you, the Self, provides the healing energy they need. To help them feel not so alone and to deepen their trust in you, it's important to consistently show up for them with messages like "I'm right here, and I'll always be here for you, no matter what—even if I get distracted or pulled away."

In addition, establishing and deepening a relationship with one part will likely have some impact on the rest of your parts. Allowing space for those other parts to express their reactions to your work with this manager may point to additional "trailheads," or places where Self-energy is blocked, as you progress on your IFS journey. You can see an example of how this happens in the following Self-led session.

Self-Led Session: Exhausted by Perfectionism

Most of us have at least some awareness of one or more of our manager parts that have taken on the role of inner critic. Many people actually have whole "teams" of critics who are completely dedicated to the project of getting us to do or be "better." While it can often be hard for us to believe, our critics are highly protective, and the only way to discover their true positive intent is to get to know them on a deeper level. To illustrate this process, I've chosen to continue working with my perfectionist part, whom I have met briefly in a previous session but don't yet know much about.

To get started, I find a comfortable space where I can sit with both feet on the floor. I sit up tall with my head aligned with my spine, taking in a few deep breaths. I soften my gaze and gently scan my body, sending some breath to several points of tension I'm sensing. This allows me to settle in more deeply.

I notice a lot of tension in my shoulders and upper back, so I bring my awareness there and the sensations intensify.

TANIS (T): "Is this you, Perfectionist part? I know from last time that you often hang out in my upper back and shoulders, and I'd like to get to know you better today if you're up for that."

PERFECTIONIST PART (P): "Yes, it is me, and that would be all right."

I ask myself how I feel toward this part there in my upper back and shoulders and immediately sense some strong annoyance toward it.

T: "OK, I'm definitely noticing you, Annoyed part—what would you like me to know right now?"

ANNOYED PART (AN): "That Perfectionist is such an incredible pain; her expectations are ridiculous, and I am so sick of it . . . she's really way too much!"

T: "It makes a lot of sense to me that you would feel that way and that you would be sick of it. Is there anything else you need me to know right now?"

AN: "Can't you just make it stop? Things would be *so* much better if she wasn't so big and trying to be in charge all the time."

T: "I completely understand that. Would it be OK with you, though, if I just got to know the Perfectionist a little better today? If you'd be willing to step back a bit, maybe I could find out more about why she needs to be this way and possibly even be able to help her."

AN: "I don't know . . . I'm worried that she'll just take over completely if I do that."

T: "I get that, too, but I have a hunch that if it's just me talking to her that she might not have to be so big. Would you be willing to at least let me try?"

AN: "Well, I guess so, but I might have to come back in if things get out of hand with her."

T: "OK, that's fair. Thank you so much for being open to letting me give it a try with her."

I sense the Annoyed one moving off to the side, and ask myself again how I feel toward the Perfectionist now . . .

I notice a clenching in my jaw and a slight fluttering sensation in my chest, so I take a couple more deep breaths, sending my awareness to those areas, and gently place one hand on my chest as I do that.

T: "I'm noticing you there in my jaw and chest. Is there something you'd like me to know about the Perfectionist part?"

JAW/CHEST PART (JC): "Absolutely! She makes me so anxious—she's really intense!"

T: "That sounds incredibly hard for you, and no wonder you're reacting the way you are. Would you be willing to let me work with her more to possibly understand her better? Maybe that could help her calm down a bit, and if we could do that it might help you, too."

ANXIOUS PART (AX): "I don't know if you can—she's very strong and can be pretty nasty . . . I don't think I can even listen if you try to talk to her."

T: "That's completely OK; you don't have to. You could go in the other room or someplace that's comfortable for you while I work with her. Would that be all right with you?"

AX: "I suppose I could do that, if you really think this will help . . . I'll go get under the covers in bed until you're done."

T: "That sounds like a good plan. I greatly appreciate you doing this so that I can get to know the Perfectionist a bit better."

I feel the tension in my jaw and chest softening and sense that the Anxious one has gone to the bedroom. I ask myself again how I feel toward the Perfectionist in my shoulders and upper back . . .

I now notice that I feel somewhat more open and a little curious toward the Perfectionist now.

T: "So, Perfectionist, I'm just curious about how you've been doing since we last met and if there's anything else you'd like me to know right now?"

PERFECTIONIST (P): "Not that great. Can't you see that I am extremely busy and don't have time for this?"

T: "Oh, well maybe you could just take a few minutes to show me more about yourself. I've certainly been feeling you in my shoulders and upper back but would like to know more. I can definitely sense how hard you're working, though."

P: "Yes, I am, and you don't seem to get it at all. There is a great deal to stay on top of here! Things *really* have to be just right and you hardly ever seem to be able to do that so I have to get after you constantly."

I ask myself again how I feel toward the Perfectionist, and I find that I am still quite curious and even somewhat concerned about her.

T: "OK, well it sounds like you really are under a lot of pressure. Would you be able to tell or show me more about this?"

I notice an image of a stern-looking woman with a tight bun, furrowed brow, and pursed lips holding a clipboard.

T: "I see you, Perfectionist, thank you so much for showing me who you are in there. You do look stressed. Would you mind telling me again what it is that you're trying to do for me right now?"

P: "Like I said, you have a real problem doing things the way they should be done even though I work so hard to make sure that everything is perfect . . . I'm just trying to keep you from messing up again."

T: "Wow, that does sound like a very big job. So, what do you think might happen if you weren't working so hard to prevent me from messing up?"

P: "Everything would just fall apart completely, and people would think that you're totally inadequate. I *have to* do this to keep that from happening and to make sure you're the best."

T: "Oh, it certainly makes sense that you wouldn't want other people to react that way, and I so appreciate how hard you work to make sure that doesn't happen. Just to help me understand you better, would you be able to tell or show me how old you are—or maybe how long you've been doing this for me?"

Now I see an image of an eight- or nine-year-old girl, clipboard in hand, looking very similar to the woman who appeared earlier.

I check to see how I feel toward this girl and notice I now feel some compassion for her.

T: "OK, I can see that you're maybe eight or nine, so you've been at this for a pretty long time. I guess I'm just wondering now what you're worried might happen if other people thought I was inadequate or if I wasn't the best?"

P: "There is *no way* that can happen! I won't let it because then you'll feel so terrible, and no one will want to be around you. They'll just see how flawed you are!"

T: "So, you're worried that I'll feel worthless or people will judge me, and then I'll be all alone, is that right?"

P: "That's exactly it, and no matter what you say, I *have to* keep pushing you to be better, to be perfect so no one can find anything to criticize."

T: "Boy, this is so much for you to have to manage, and I want to reassure you that I don't expect you to stop doing this. I see how important this is and would just like to be with you if that's OK?"

P: "Well, you're right, it is tough, but I really have no choice."

T: "I totally get that. How does it feel to you that I'm here with you right now?"

P: "I guess it's OK—it helps that you're at least trying to understand, even though I'm not so sure that you can."

T: "I know. It makes a lot of sense to me that you're not so sure about me yet, and I think it'll just take some time. I'm just curious—how old do you think I am?"

P: "Maybe four or five."

T: "Well, I can understand how you might think that. I probably messed up a lot when I was that age! But actually, I've been an adult for quite some time now so I can really be here in a different way for you now."

P: "That's crazy—I had no idea."

T: "It's OK—seems like you're pretty wrapped up in this demanding job of yours so it would be hard for you to know. Another thing I'm wondering is how you feel toward me?"

P: "You seem OK, and it is nice to have someone to talk to."

T: "I'm glad to hear that you feel that way. Is there anything else you'd like to know about me?"

P: "Hmm . . . I can't think of anything right now, but maybe I will later."

T: "Sounds good. Is there anything more you'd like me to know right now or anything you need that maybe I could help you with?"

P: "I don't think so. I just have to keep making sure you don't mess up."

T: "I get it, and I was just thinking about that, too. How do you feel about this difficult role you're in? Do you like having to do things this way?"

P: "Not really, but I have to keep doing it."

T: "I know, and I'm really concerned that you feel so stuck. Is there more to it for you in terms of the other parts inside? Are there things that go on with any of them that make it even more challenging for you?"

P: "Definitely. You heard that really Annoyed one, and the Anxious one earlier, right? The Annoyed one fights with me a lot, and the Anxious one just runs around wringing its hands. They do make things much harder for me, but I'm used to it by now, so I just try to ignore or criticize them so they'll stop."

T: "That does sound very difficult for you. How do the other two parts react when you criticize or ignore them?"

P: "Sometimes the Anxious one will cry and go away for a while, but then it's worse later, and the Annoyed one usually just gets pretty angry."

T: "Wow, that sounds really rough . . ."

P: "It is, but there isn't any other way, and that's why I have to get so big sometimes. I am getting tired of all of it, though."

T: "I would think you would be with *everything* you're trying to stay on top of in there. You said earlier that if you weren't doing all of it that I'd feel so bad and no one would want to be around me. Does that have anything to do with another part you're connected to—maybe someone you're trying to protect?"

P: "I think so, but all I know is that one feels *really* awful most of the time, and I have to keep doing this so it doesn't feel even worse and totally takes over."

T: "Oh, it sounds like making sure that doesn't happen is the reason you have to keep doing all this. No wonder you're working so hard! I am truly amazed by how committed you are to taking care of things this way. I have such deep respect for you and your role in the system, even though I know now how hard it is for you with these other parts."

P: "That's good, and you're right—it is pretty tough."

T: "I know. Do you feel like it's been helpful to you that we've been able to spend this time together today?"

P: "Pretty much—I do like talking to you."

T: "That's great. Would you like to do this more regularly, and if you do, how would you like that to be?"

P: "That might be good—maybe checking in like this at the end of the day, a couple times a week or something like that?"

T: "OK, I'll jot that down, and we'll plan on it. Just remember that I'm always here for you, though, so we can also reconnect pretty much whenever you need to. Maybe I could help you with those other parts a little bit. Would that be reasonable?"

P: "Oh, yes, it would. They really cause a lot of problems for me, so if you could talk to them, too, maybe they could settle down."

T: "That's an excellent idea, and I'm really grateful you've been able to be so open with me today. I've learned quite a lot. I know it wasn't easy for you at first and that it took some courage to hang in there with me."

P: "You're right, and I'm glad you're here and are finally listening to me."

T: "Of course, and before we wrap it up, would it be OK if we just check back with the Annoyed and Anxious parts for a minute?"

P: "Yeah, that's OK with me."

T: "So, Annoyed and Anxious ones, are you still around?"

AX & AN: "Yes, we're here."

T: "Great. I just wanted to thank you again for being willing to step back earlier and allowing me to do this work with the Perfectionist today. How was this for you, if you were listening, and is there anything you're concerned about before we stop for right now?"

AN: "I was definitely listening, and I'm pretty surprised by the whole thing. I had no idea that the Perfectionist feels so stuck, but when she gets going, it's nearly impossible not to try to get her to stop."

AX: "I feel the same way—I'm worried that now that you've talked to her she might be even stronger."

T: "Those are very good points, you two. Perfectionist, do you think you'll need to be stronger now that you and I have gotten to know each other a bit?"

P: "Not necessarily, because maybe now I can just talk to you when I'm upset or something, but I might not be able to help it sometimes."

T: "I know, and we can keep working on it together. How would it be if I also spend some time with you, Anxious and Annoyed parts? I'm thinking all three of you could use some more support and care."

AN: "I don't know, but we could try it out. I don't think I really need any help, though."

T: "I get it, but I'd just like to get to know you anyway, if that would be OK. How about you, Anxious one?"

AX: "I would really like that— sometimes everything just feels overwhelming."

T: "It really does sound like it, and I'd like to hear more about that. How about you and I have some time together soon, and I can check in with the Annoyed one, too, just to see how things are?"

AX: "Yes, whatever you can do. I can see that it's been good for the Perfectionist to talk with you."

AN: "Agreed."

T: "Well, thank you all for doing this with me today. It means a lot to me. So, I'll check in with you, Perfectionist, in a few days to see how you're doing. If you're still up for it, Anxious one, we can also spend time together. And I will check back with you, Annoyed one; at some point you and I can get to know each other better as well. It's been really great having this time with all of you."

P, AX & AN: "OK, see you later then."

T: "Absolutely; see you soon."

Manager Meditation

What You'll Need

- 20 to 40 minutes of uninterrupted time
- A recording device
- A journal, sketchpad, or digital notebook (if desired)
- Pen, colored pencils, or markers (if desired)

Overview

Guided meditations assist us on our Self-led IFS journey by inviting us to slow down and tune in as fully as we can to our inner world, which always includes our parts if that is our intention for the practice. In this way, we can gently unblend from and be more present with our parts as well as offer a welcoming space for them to share themselves with us in whatever way feels right to them in the moment. It may be helpful to record yourself reading this meditation aloud or have someone read it to you so that you can stay in the experience, and once you're in it, feel free to let go of the suggested prompts and follow your internal guidance for what feels best to your own internal system as you spend this time with some of your helpful managers.

Instructions

1. Set yourself up in a comfortable position, sitting up tall but not rigid or tense, or lie down. Take several slow, deep breaths.

2. Allow your breath to carry you inward, closing your eyes or softening your gaze, noticing your body's points of contact with the chair, floor, or bed. Also notice any sensations of energy moving through your body, areas that are tight or tense, the state of your heart (does it feel soft, tight, open, loving), or anything else that draws your attention.

3. Notice if there are any thoughts or feelings present, offering them a calming breath or two as you do.

4. Gently inquire whether any of the bodily sensations, thoughts, or feelings present are a part or parts, and if you get the sense that they are, see if you can tell how you feel toward them.

5. Ask if there are one or two who might like to spend some time with you now. If so, and if no other parts are reacting to them, extend some curiosity and compassion to them.

6. As you are focusing on this part or parts, just let them know that you're aware that they work very hard for you. Ask what they might like to share with you right now about that, in whatever way they can (this might be in words, images, body sensations, or memories), and thank them for whatever comes.

7. Ask them now, if it feels right, to let you know what they're trying to do for you by working so hard in their roles, also reassuring them that if they don't feel up to saying much at the present time regarding this, that is perfectly OK.

8. Notice if it feels possible to open your heart to this part or parts even more, and ask what more this part or parts might need to feel fully seen and acknowledged by you.

9. See if you can continue sending gratitude to this part or parts for all the work they do for you every day. Ask if they would be open to helping you become more aware of how they are helping you attend to things in your daily life.

10. Now, ask if there is a particular way this part or parts wants to be known by you. This can be in the form of an image or color, a name to refer to them by, etc.

11. Let this part(s) know how much you value its commitment to you and the whole internal family system and that you'd like to continue getting to know them moving forward if that would be OK.

12. While taking a few more slow, deep breaths, offer this part your love and appreciation for just being with you, and then say good-bye for now. If you wish, you can reinforce your appreciation with soothing physical gestures. Record anything in your journal that feels important about what was revealed to you in this experience.

My Manager's Story

What You'll Need

- 20 to 40 minutes of uninterrupted time
- Blank paper, a journal, or sketchpad
- Pen, colored pencils, or markers

Overview

Increasing our awareness of *all* that our managers hold for us and more thoroughly understanding their "story" helps us to continue to bring more compassion and healing to them. That is the intention of this letter-writing exercise. It can be particularly effective when you are first getting to know your managers. You can also use it with any of your other parts.

Instructions

1. Position yourself in a space that is both comfortable and in which you can easily write, with your blank paper, journal, sketchpad, and pen or markers handy.

2. Take a few deep breaths, turning your attention inward and noticing whatever you can in or around your body as you do.

3. If you can already tell that there is a part or parts present, tune into them. If not, see if you can bring to your awareness a part that is very present in your life. Perhaps it is one that:

   - Takes care of or helps others a good deal of the time.
   - Works hard to get things done or get things "right."
   - Worries a lot or is judgmental, critical, or strives to be perfect.
   - Keeps you really organized and task-oriented.
   - Enjoys achieving, making sure you do everything necessary to reach your goals.
   - Keeps you busy working all the time.

4. You may find it helpful now to consider a recent situation in which a part like this was involved, and if one does emerge, see how you notice it. Can you hear its voice or thoughts? Do you see an image, color, or shape connected to it or mostly sense it in a particular place in your body?

5. Once you're focusing on your manager part, ask yourself how you feel toward it. If you find that other parts are reacting to it, listen to and validate their concerns, and then respectfully ask them to step back.

6. Let this part know how you feel toward it once the other parts have unblended, allowing there to be a bit of space between you and this part. Extend your appreciation to it in whatever way feels right.

7. Now, ask this part if it would help you by sharing more of its story with you in the form of a letter to you. Let it know that, if it would be helpful, it can also use color and images in this letter (and can use your colored pencils/markers for this).

8. Ask it to include in this letter all the things that might be difficult about its job and what frustrates it about its role in your system, in your relationships, or in external situations (e.g., your work, other demands on your time, or people that get on its nerves). Ask it to write about other parts that it has issues with or that it worries about, etc. Encourage it to keep writing until its "story" to you for today feels complete.

9. Once the part finishes its letter, be sure to thank it. Then, from your larger perspective of care, curiosity, clarity, compassion, and calm, write back to it, addressing the concerns it has raised.

10. If it feels helpful, read your letter aloud to your part, noting its response as it feels right.

11. Extend your gratitude for all that this part does for you, noting specific aspects of its story and asking if there is anything more it would like to share with you before completing this exercise.

12. Make note of what you've learned in your journal if you'd like. Draw an image of this part if that's helpful, and say goodbye to it for now, letting it know that this conversation can continue anytime.

EXERCISE 3
Manager Mapping

What You'll Need

- 20 to 40 minutes of uninterrupted time
- A large piece of blank paper, a sketchpad, or journal
- Colored pencils, markers, or a pen

Overview

A powerful way to identify and externalize a "cluster" of the parts in our internal family system is to create a map of them. You may find this useful as you continue to work to unblend from and further deepen your relationships with your "team" of managers. This can help you visualize the internal relationships they have both with one another and with you, the Self. It can also reveal particular patterns that play out among them over time as well (though you may need to revise the map as you learn more). Allow your managers to guide you with the ways in which they want to be depicted on your map. Remember that this representation can take shape in whatever way makes sense for you (and them!). It can be more of a diagram with lots of writing, it might be more artistic with colors and images/shapes, or it could be a unique combination of the two.

Instructions

1. Settle into a comfortable place where you can write or draw easily, and take several deep breaths.

2. Turn your attention inside and ask that any of the managers you've already met and have been working with be present with you now. If you don't notice any parts emerging initially, check in with your body to see what parts might be drawing your awareness.

3. Note how you feel toward these parts. Listen to the concerns of any other parts that may be reacting to them and then ask them to kindly relax if they can; let them know that they can be part of this experience, too, if they'd like.

4. Draw a symbol, sign, design, or shape that can represent you (the Self), placing this somewhere near the center of the page. This could be a circle, a heart, or whatever feels right.

5. Now, focus again on the part or parts that are present and check with them to see how and where they'd like to be depicted on the page. Consider the following:

   • What type of symbol, shape, or image would they like to appear as?
   • Where in relation to the Self do they want to be?
   • Do they want to use colors, designs, or words to express who they are on the map?
   • Would they like you to write in their name or what their role is in some way?

6. Write or draw whatever your managers express about themselves on your map. Also ask how they would like the relationships between them to be shown there. Are they close to one another, or to you, or far apart? Should there be any indication of particular boundaries or special connections between them?

7. Continue to fill in the map with these parts until it feels complete for now. Ask them if there is any story they feel should go with it, or any other parts that they are connected to that should be there as well.

8. Thank these parts for everything they shared in this process. Even if only one part participated in this activity, you can continue to add to this map as you come to know more of your parts over time.

9. Look at your "manager map" and reflect on what you notice either on the page or in your journal.

CHAPTER FIVE

Working with Your Firefighter Parts

You've now arrived at the point in your Self-led IFS journey where you'll more thoroughly explore the nature of your firefighters. These are the parts of us that are most often misunderstood due to their impulsive and risk-taking behaviors, but they are also the ones focused on providing relief and comfort from distress and pain. This chapter will guide you through the process of deepening both your relationships with and your understanding of this fascinating group of parts that make up the other side of the internal protective system.

Understanding Firefighter Parts

While they share the common goal of protecting the system, our managers and firefighters couldn't be more different in their approach. Because they are reactive by nature and focused on acting "in the moment" with little regard for the impact of their actions, our firefighters tend to invite opposition from the managers. As their name implies, however, these parts of us play a vital role in safeguarding the system by immediately responding to either extinguish or divert attention away from the emotional flames that an exile is experiencing, thereby protecting both that part and the entire system from being engulfed by that fire.

Similar to our managers, firefighters are tireless in these efforts and wholly dedicate themselves to both neutralizing the threat of potential emotional devastation and calming the distress of an activated exile. Roles our firefighters typically adopt include the procrastinator, the zoned-out social media/internet scroller, television-watcher, or video-gamer, as well as our annoyed, angry, or enraged parts. Rebellious, daydreaming, or fantasizing parts are also included in the firefighter group, as are those that overeat, drink, spend, or use other substances and experiences (such as sex or gambling) to numb and distract. Obsessively working, organizing, cleaning, and even isolating to avoid the risk of exposing vulnerability are behaviors our firefighters can take on as well. Depending on the degree or severity of the emotional burdens carried by the exiles they protect, their "acting out" behaviors can range from mildly distracting (and still relatively socially acceptable) to debilitating and extreme, such as addiction, abusive tendencies, and self-harm.

Understandably, our managers have little tolerance for the firefighters' protective strategies because they've had to deal with the repercussions of their actions on a fairly regular basis. They therefore tend to both blame and shame them for causing *more* problems, which can often intensify the firefighters' efforts to continue to do their jobs, no matter the cost. This is a setup for friction and conflict between them as the firefighters impulsively (and often compulsively) act to prevent what they perceive will be massive emotional floods or raging fires from completely overtaking us. They truly believe that they *have to* rush into service to provide either some temporary relief from discomfort or a sense of control as a means to avoid the pain, and they are convinced there is no other way to accomplish this.

From the firefighters' perspective, this approach to protection is highly effective, and when met with compassion, they will often tell us that their actual desire is to help give us a break from the difficulty and pain of life, along with the boredom they believe would result from only following what our managers want us to do. In a piece entitled "Why I Love My Firefighters," longtime IFS senior trainer, clinician, and mentor Cece Sykes writes: "It is the vibrance and carefree enthusiasm of firefighter energy that adds sparkle and spice to the humdrum . . . without flouting convention every once in a while, without taking a few chances, life would become a crushing bore."

So, what our firefighters most need to begin to heal is our genuine appreciation, understanding, and acceptance for all that they offer us, as well as for the difficult dilemmas they face. They are clearly not at all what they appear to be at first glance, so when they can finally feel heard and known by *us*, in Self-energy, without the influence of the managers that are so reactive to them, they are able to reveal their true nature and intent. This in itself can be incredibly healing and new for them, as they are quite accustomed to being misunderstood and sometimes characterized as abnormal, both internally and externally. They also need our assistance intervening in the often-heated conflicts (which we refer to in IFS as polarizations) that naturally occur between them and the managers. Without the mediating support of Self-energy, these cycles of conflict often escalate and can then cause both sides to become more extreme.

While it may be difficult for them to admit initially, our firefighters don't want to remain locked in these defensive struggles. However, because they tend to be our inner teenagers, they also have no idea how to extricate themselves from them either. So, to truly transform and step into the more harmonious roles that they would actually prefer, our firefighters need the exiles they protect to become unburdened so there is no longer such a threat of those emotional fires breaking out.

Tips for Working with Firefighter Parts

Increasing our *awareness* of the often subtle or somewhat unconscious ways our firefighters operate in the system is vital for establishing more collaborative relationships with them. To do this, it is extremely important to continuously work to unblend from managers that polarize with them. Firefighters are very sensitive to and understandably resentful of any whiff of management or controlling energy in our interactions with them, since this is what they must contend with constantly from the managers.

Therefore, in our work with firefighters, our priorities are to offer them our sincere appreciation for their urgent need to protect us, to acknowledge how valuable both their energy and sacrifices are to us, and to assist them with their challenging relationships with the managers. When we can nurture our connections with our firefighters from a place of curiosity, understanding, and compassion, we celebrate them for their desire to help us enjoy and live our lives more fully as well.

Step One: Reconnect with My Firefighter Part(s)

This step involves inviting a part or parts that you may have encountered in the previous chapter to continue your work together. It may be that the "target part" you met in chapter 3 was one of your firefighters, and this is an opportunity to begin the process of learning more about it.

Instructions

1. Settle into a comfortable space, sitting up tall or lying down, and take in a few slow, deep breaths.

2. Turn your awareness inward, closing your eyes or softening your gaze if that's helpful to you. Tune into whatever sensations or points of tension are present in your body. As you do, send some breaths to those places.

3. Gently ask if there is a firefighter part or parts that want to distract your attention away from discomfort, pain, or stress you may be experiencing that would like your attention now. Or ask if the firefighter you previously met would like to reconnect.

4. Notice if an image, voice, or heightened bodily sensation arises, and let it know that you are present with it.

5. See if you can tell how you feel toward whatever shows up, and if this isn't something like curious, open, compassionate, neutral, caring, or interested, check in with whatever other part or parts might be reacting to this one. Acknowledge and validate its concerns, and ask it if it will step back a bit and not interrupt while you work with the first part.

6. Check again to determine how you feel toward your target part, and repeat the previous step until you are present with it from a place of compassion, curiosity, kindness, concern, or openness.

7. Now, gently inquire about how this part has been doing since you met with it last time (if it is that part), and if there is anything else it would like you to know right now. If this part is not the same one that you met earlier, ask it to let you know more about itself in whatever way feels right.

8. Write down anything the part tells you in your journal if that feels helpful.

TIP: For assistance with this step, try out "Firefighter Awareness" on page 138 or go back to "Getting to Know Your Parts" on page 83.

Step Two: Deepen the Dialogue with This Firefighter Part

Once our firefighters sense they have our undivided attention and that we will listen fully to them in all their complexity, their trust in us grows. Therefore, the intention of this step is to continue developing awareness and understanding of the firefighter you've just established contact with.

Instructions

1. Continue the conversation you began with this firefighter in the previous step, asking any follow-up questions that come to you based on what it has been able to share with you so far.

2. Ask yourself again how you *feel toward* this part to check for other reactive parts and to determine the degree to which you are still in Self as you engage with this part.

3. If other parts are reacting, acknowledge and validate their concerns and then respectfully ask that they step back so you can continue working with this part. Thank them for doing so.

4. Gently ask this part to remind you what it feels that its job is or what it is trying to accomplish for you. Once it lets you know this, follow up with any clarifying questions that feel necessary so that you can fully understand what it means. Reflect your understanding back to this part if that feels right.

5. Now, ask this part if it can tell or show you about how old it is and at what point in your life it stepped into this role, again asking for clarification if needed.

6. Reassure your firefighter that it has all the time and space it needs to let you know these things—that it's not necessary for its responses to come quickly, or at all, and that you are just hoping to understand it more completely as you spend time with it here.

7. Check again with this part to see if there is more it would like to share regarding the concerns it has if it wasn't doing this job or if it even relaxed a little in this role. Again, reflect back to it what it tells you to make sure you understand fully.

8. Gently inquire if there is anything else this firefighter would like you to know about its story or what it tries to do to help the internal system overall.

9. Extend your gratitude for all this part has been able to share with you in this step.

TIP: For additional support with this step, try out "Firefighter Awareness" on page 138 and "The Fire Drill" on page 140.

Step Three: Establish a Two-Way Relationship with This Firefighter Part

When our parts come to know us more fully, they can begin to trust that *we* are safe, can be present and attend to them in whatever ways they may need, and can be depended upon to help them now. Therefore, the purpose of this step is to continue deepening your relationship with this part by checking in with it regarding its awareness of *you*, the Self.

Instructions

1. As your conversation continues to unfold with this firefighter, let it know that you're curious about how it feels toward *you*, the Self, and whether or not it can *feel* you there with it right now.

2. If it doesn't quite know yet how to respond to this, reassure it that it makes sense that it might need space to "feel out" this connection with you and that it will likely take some time for the relationship between you to develop, which is totally OK and understandable.

3. Depending on how it responds to you, you can also ask this part how old it thinks you are (which will likely be a much younger age than you are now). Then either tell it or show it the age you actually are now.

4. Discuss its reaction to this together, checking to see if there is more this part would like to know about you.

5. If it feels intuitively right, ask this firefighter how it feels to know that you are present and spending time with it now and if there is anything it needs or would like your support with.

TIP: For assistance with this step, try out "The Fire Drill" on page 140.

Step Four: Gain a Deeper Understanding of This Firefighter's Role

The goal of this step is to expand your awareness of the role this firefighter plays in your system overall, including the nature of its relationships with other parts and the constraints it may feel as a result of these relationships.

Instructions

1. As you continue to sit with this firefighter part, ask it how it feels about its job: Does it *like* this role, and are there aspects of it that make things particularly difficult for it?

2. Encourage the part to express to you as much as it can about what might be hard for it within the system overall. Is there more it wants to say about this?

3. Inquire now about this firefighter's *relationships* with other parts: How does it feel toward or get along with the parts that may have been reactive to it at the beginning of this session (or when you first met it)? Can it tell you anything more about other parts it may be particularly allied with or in conflict with?

4. Offer reassurance to your firefighter, again, that your hope is to become increasingly *aware* of how all the parts inside are interrelated and work together, and that if it doesn't feel ready or able to discuss these things right now, you understand and are confident that you will come to know this over time.

5. Now, ask your firefighter if it might be able to let you know anything about the part or parts that it protects. It may have alluded to this when asked about its concerns regarding what might happen if it wasn't doing its job or even relaxed in its work a bit. Invite it here to clarify whether these concerns are connected to

a specific vulnerable part that it protects (it may or may not have full awareness of this, which is totally fine).

6. Extend your gratitude for all that this firefighter has been able to share with you in this step. If you wish, you can reinforce this gratitude with whatever physical gesture feels appropriate. Jot down what you've learned in your journal for later reference.

> TIP: Helpful exercises for this step are "The Fire Drill" on page 140 and "Firefighter Mapping" on page 143.

Step Five: Invite Continued Collaboration and Conclude the Session with This Firefighter Part

The intention of this step is to integrate what you've learned from this part and to express your desire to continue a collaborative relationship with it. Because being with you in this way is initially an unfamiliar experience, it is powerful and necessary at this point to offer your continued presence and gratitude to this part (and the other parts that tend to react to it) for the commitment and courage it has shown during this session.

Instructions

1. If it feels helpful to review what this firefighter has expressed to you about its role, concerns, and its relationships with other parts in your internal family system, go ahead and do that now.

2. Reiterate your deep appreciation and respect for everything this part does for you and its position in your internal family,

acknowledging the courage it took for it to engage with you more fully during this time.

3. Ask this part (along with the parts that stepped back so that you could work with this one) whether it feels that this time together has been helpful to it and how it would like to stay connected with you.

4. Reflecting on some of the specific difficulties this part has shared with you that it experiences in its role, inquire if it might like some assistance or support from you with those concerns and how it feels you could best help.

5. Now invite this part (along with any others that stepped back initially) to let you know if it would like you to check in with it in a particular way moving forward (e.g., every day, at a particular time of day, a couple of times a week, or whenever you notice it), and if it does, make a note of that.

6. Say goodbye for the time being and indicate your intention to follow through with staying connected to both this firefighter and any other parts you had contact with in this session in order to continue to strengthen your ongoing relationships with them.

TIP: For further support and reflection in this step, check out "Firefighter Mapping" on page 143.

Self-Led Session: Struggling with Impulse Control

Whether or not we're able to notice them, most everyone has parts that do their jobs by distracting or pulling us off track in some way. When we have little awareness of what those parts are really about, we often stay blended with one or more of our managers who react to such behaviors with irritation and attempts to control them. This is exactly the scenario I've decided to explore in this session, as I reconnect with a distractor part I briefly encountered in some previous work and that I've been noticing a bit more since that time.

I begin by sitting up tall in a comfortable and quiet space with both feet grounded on the floor. I close my eyes and check in with my body as I slow down my breathing, noticing the rise and fall of my belly. As I do this, I begin to notice a slight buzzing in my head and a "jumpy" sensation in my gut. I send some breaths to these areas, and I feel myself settling in a little more.

I keep sending deep breaths to both my head and gut, and as I do, the buzzing in my head increases slightly.

TANIS (T): "I'm definitely noticing you there in my head and also that there is something going on in my belly. OK if I hear from the head part first?"

I notice that the jumpiness in my belly actually settles a tiny bit, while the buzzing remains.

I ask myself how I feel toward the buzzing one in my head. I find that I feel fairly open to it, and I realize that I recognize it as a manager I've met before.

T: "I'm getting the sense that's you, Head part. It's been a while since we've talked."

HEAD PART (H): "It has, and there's plenty going on in here that you should know about."

T: "OK, would you like to tell me more?"

H: "Definitely . . . I am absolutely beyond frustrated that you have so much to do and you're not doing it. You're just goofing off a lot of the time."

T: "Hmm . . . well, I can certainly understand why you'd be frustrated by that. I remember from our talk before that you are very concerned about making sure I stay focused and work hard. Is there more you'd like me to know about that?"

H: "Yes, I would because you just don't seem to get it! If things keep going the way they are, you'll never get that big project done that you've been trying to finish now for weeks—you just keep getting sidetracked all the time, and if that keeps happening, you'll never make it, and I just can't let that happen. So I have to make sure you keep working really hard on it, but you're letting that other one take over."

T: "OK, that makes a lot of sense; you're all about making sure I stay on task, and I know you have a lot of worries about what might happen if I don't. I so appreciate all you're doing to make sure I get that project done, but I am also wondering if it would be OK with

you if I talk to that one you just mentioned. Maybe if I did it would make things somewhat easier for you, too."

H: "Well, I guess that might be all right if you promise not to let her take over completely. She's pretty unpredictable, and if she has her way, you'd just be lounging around doing nothing all the time."

T: "I get it, and I promise I won't let her get bigger. I'd just like to understand her better, which actually might help the entire situation. Would you be willing to step off to the side a bit and not interrupt as I talk with her?"

H: "I guess I could do that, but you'd better be careful; she's pretty chaotic and all."

T: "Thank you, I appreciate your concern about that and that you're OK with letting me be with her."

I notice the Head part softening and that the buzzing has faded away. I get the sense the jumpiness in my stomach might be this part, so I focus my attention there.

As I do this, the jumpiness revs up a little again, and I ask myself how I feel toward it. I notice that I now feel quite interested and curious toward this one in my belly.

T: "Hello, Jumpy part . . . I'm just wondering how you've been doing since we met last and if there's something going on that has you kind of active right now?"

JUMPY PART (J): "I'm OK, but that Head part just makes things really hard."

T: "Yes, I'm beginning to see that the two of you don't get along so well, which *would* make things hard for you. Could you tell me more about what it is that you're trying to do for me right now?"

J: "Yeah, I guess. I get so sick of you working all the time—I'm just trying to give you a break by watching Netflix and stuff because everything is so stressful."

T: "Oh, that makes sense; it sounds like you want me to have some downtime because I've been working too much."

J: "Yeah, and Head part is always on my back about it, so I've been having to do it more lately. Otherwise you would never stop working . . ."

T: "Well, you do have a good point there. I'm curious, could you tell or show me about how old you are?"

J: "I'm fourteen, and I just *have to* pull you away from being so serious all the time!"

T: "So what do you think might happen if you weren't doing that so much right now?"

J: "You'd fall into the pit of sadness."

T: "Hmm . . . I certainly get why you wouldn't want that to happen. Is there more you'd like to share with me right now?"

J: "I don't know—we should just go watch Netflix instead of doing this. That would be way more fun."

T: "Oh, I get it, and that does sound like fun. But I'd really like to keep getting to know you a little better if that's OK."

J: "I guess so, but I might have to go if it gets too boring."

T: "I understand, but I hope that won't happen since I'm getting the sense that there's a lot more to you than it seems like at first, and I know that things aren't necessarily so easy for you in there . . ."

J: "That's right."

T: "So how does it feel to you that I'm here with you right now, and how old do you think I am?"

J: "It feels OK. I'm glad you're here because at least right now Head part is off my back. I think you're maybe nineteen or something like that."

T: "Well, that's a really good guess, but I'm actually much older than that—I've been an adult for quite some time now."

J: "That's too bad—I think it really stinks to have to be an adult and have to just work and work and be so serious all the time."

T: "You definitely have a good point there. It can be hard sometimes with work and lots of responsibilities, but not all the time. How do you think you came to believe that about having to be so serious all the time when you're a grown-up?"

J: "I could just tell. You and your friends had to start working super hard in school because those manager parts pushed you to get straight As, and it seemed like Mom and Dad were pretty stressed having to work so much."

T: "You're right—it was kind of like that then, but there were still times when we had fun."

J: "Yeah, because of *me*. I couldn't stand the way those managers were on you all the time, so I had to jump in—I'm the Fun Girl."

T: "So you've been doing this for a pretty long time, huh? And is that what you'd like me to call you, Fun Girl? Seems like you've been very creative in finding ways to release some of the pressure, and I so appreciate everything you do to help me. I have noticed that we're kind of zoning out binging on Netflix more lately, though. Is there a reason you've ramped things up recently?"

FUN GIRL (F): "Yes, you can call me that, and I've had no choice but to make you binge on Netflix more—those managers are getting really nasty, and I just *have* to!"

T: "Oh boy, that sounds really tough for you. Do you like having to do your job this way? It seems like it might create some stress for you, too."

F: "Yeah, it does when the managers are this bad, but I just end up sneaking in when they're not paying attention to take you out of that crazy work mode for a while."

T: "I know, and lately it has been for longer stretches of time. What happens when Head part and the other managers realize what's been going on?"

F: "Oh, they just get more mad and stomp around . . ."

T: "That must be a little tricky for you—what happens then?"

F: "I just try to ignore them or hang out with a couple others in here who're on my side."

T: "OK, so I'm beginning to see more clearly why they've been more upset, and you've had to pull me out more. I think I already have a pretty good idea, but how do you feel toward Head part and the other managers?"

F: "They're a total pain in the butt and are always trying to control me, which I *really* hate."

T: "I get that—sounds like it can get pretty tense between you all. You said earlier that you do what you do so that I won't fall into the pit of sadness. Could you tell me a little more about that?"

F: "All I know is that it would be *really* bad—like it would feel like you would die from feeling like a total failure or something. I've been noticing that trying to bubble up more lately, and I have to make sure it stays down there and doesn't get out."

T: "Wow, now I can totally see why you've had to be more active if that's been triggered, and I can't tell you how grateful I am to you that you've been able to share so much with me about this, and for how hard you're working to make sure that doesn't happen."

F: "It's OK. Like I said, I've been doing this for a long time, and I just want you to feel good once in a while."

T: "I really appreciate that, too, and I have a great deal of respect for you trying to balance out the managers while you're also taking care of that other one that feels so awful. It seems like that's a lot for you."

F: "Yeah, it really is sometimes."

T: "How has it been for you that we're talking about this together now, and would you like to stay more connected with me so that I can hear more about how things are for you?"

F: "It's good to have you here with me so I can feel like someone understands—those managers sure don't!"

T: "Would you like some help with that? Maybe next time I could meet with both you and Head part to see if we can maybe ease up the tension on both sides. What do you think?"

F: "I think that might help, but I don't know if they'll cooperate."

T: "I know, and that's OK—we can see about that when the time comes. But, for now, is there a particular way you'd like me to check in with you in the next week or so?"

F: "OK, maybe when you take a break from working. I can try not to make you zone out so much if you can take more breaks . . ."

T: "That sounds really good, and so that I have a better idea of what's going on inside, maybe you can also let me know when you are starting to feel the need to shut down the overworking. How would that be?"

F: "Yeah, that would probably be good—I'd appreciate that."

T: "Well, I really appreciate you for being open to these ideas and for the courage it took to hang in there with me today, and for *all* that you do—thank you. Is there anything else you'd like me to know before we're done for now?"

F: "You got it, and yeah . . . one other reason I try to get you away from all the stress sometimes is so that you'll have the energy you need to get that project done—otherwise those managers would totally run you into the ground."

T: "Wow, that's very wise, and it helps me a great deal to know that. I'll definitely plan to check in with you in a couple of days, OK?"

F: "Yeah, that would be good."

T: "Great. Now I think it might be a good idea to check back in with Head part, if that's OK?"

F: "I guess it is—she's probably been listening anyway."

T: "Thank you. Head part, are you still around, and how do you think it went with Fun Girl?"

H: "Yes, I'm here, and I'm very surprised. I had no idea she was actually trying to help by doing this. It's still aggravating, but now it makes a little more sense at least."

T: "I'm glad to hear that, Head part, and I'm not sure if you heard, but Fun Girl and I were thinking it might be helpful for the three of us to get together sometime soon to talk about the tension between you. Do you think you might be OK with that?"

H: "Maybe, this fighting really does make everything harder, and I can now see that this isn't just about goofing off . . ."

T: "Great, so let's plan on doing that soon, OK? I'd really like to help you both ease up a bit if that's possible, and I thank you for being open to it."

H: "OK, but I will probably still get mad at her when she's doing that a lot."

T: "I understand—one step at a time. Thank you both so much, and I'll check back in with you soon."

F & H: "OK, see you then."

Firefighter Awareness

What You'll Need

- 20 to 40 minutes of uninterrupted time
- Blank paper, a journal, sketchpad, or digital notebook
- Pen, colored pencils, or markers

Overview

It can be more challenging to identify and notice our firefighters than our managers because firefighters are generally present only when the pain of an exile has been triggered or there's a perceived threat of this occurring. We can, however, start to become aware of our firefighters by tapping into our intuition to uncover the typical strategies they have used with us over time. In this exercise, you will explore the various roles your firefighters may occupy in your internal family system to better recognize and connect with them.

Instructions

1. Settle into a comfortable position where you can write or draw easily, and take a few slow, deep breaths.

2. Spend a moment noticing any thoughts or sensations (which may be coming from parts), and whether you're otherwise aware of any parts that may be present.

3. If you do notice any parts, let them know that their input is welcome and that you want to know as much as you can about your firefighters. If any managers are present, ask that they try not to judge or be reactive if possible.

4. Now, begin to list or draw some of your firefighters that could show up in the following ways:

    - **Self-soothing parts:** Those that seek temporary relief from emotional pain or stress through food, substances, sleeping, shopping, etc.
    - **Distracting parts:** Those that distract through binge-watching TV, mindless social media scrolling, video games, staying busy, etc.
    - **Anger/rage parts:** Those that use anger and irritation to distract from emotional pain.
    - **Escapist parts:** Those that try to escape reality by day-dreaming or other forms of spacing out.

5. As you make your lists, brainstorm as much as possible and try not to be concerned about getting it "right."

6. When your list feels complete, read it over and then take some time to journal about what you notice.

The Fire Drill

What You'll Need

- 20 to 40 minutes of uninterrupted time
- A recording device (if desired)
- Your journal, sketchpad, or digital notebook
- Pen, colored pencils, or markers if desired

Overview

This exercise was created by Dr. Richard C. Schwartz in collaboration with Hakomi Method developer Ron Kurtz. It has been used for many years in the IFS community to practice and become more aware of unblending from reactive parts in the midst of an upsetting situation. To facilitate bringing more Self-energy into the experience, this practice helps you "rehearse" for moments when your protectors (fire-fighters or other reactive parts, which can include managers) are provoked. You may wish to record yourself reading these instructions or have someone read the instructions to you so that it's easier to stay in the experience as it unfolds.

Instructions

1. Sit or lie down in a comfortable position, and take a few slow, deep breaths, noticing any points of tension, thoughts, or feelings that may be present.

2. Offer calming breaths to those sensations and inquire whether any parts have concerns about this practice. If so, acknowledge and validate them, and reassure these parts that this practice will be helpful and, if needed, you can return to them later to work with their reactions.

3. Now, bring to mind a person from your past or present who triggers a strong reaction in you (e.g., someone who frustrates you, someone who you feel criticized by, or someone who

really makes you angry). Imagine this person alone in a room where they must stay for right now. Look at this person through a window so you can see them doing or saying the things that upset you.

4. Notice what happens with your breathing, heart, muscles, feelings, and thoughts as one or more of your protector parts react. Look again at this person and notice how they appear to you through the eyes of this protector.

5. Ask this protector if it's willing to allow a bit of separation between itself and you right now, since you will not have it confront this person in any way. Reassure this part that it's safe with you and that you won't enter the room containing this person.

6. If your protector has been able to unblend at least a little, see if you can notice any changes in how your body feels now—what's happening with your breathing, heart, muscles, feelings, and thoughts? Take another look at the provoking person. Do they appear any differently to you now?

7. See if you can shift your focus back to your protector. Can you become even more curious about it now that there is some separation between you? If so, ask this protector *why* it feels such a need to react so strongly to this person. Also ask what it's afraid would happen if it didn't react in this way for you. Extend some gratitude to it for taking care of you in the way that it does. Ask if it would like to continue to discuss its role and concerns either now or at a later time.

8. Now, ask this part, hypothetically, what it might be like if you enter the room from this more Self-led place so that it wouldn't have to be the one dealing with this person? What might that look and feel like, both to you and to this part? How might this play out in terms of how you might now relate to this person?

9. If you do get a sense of how this experience would be different with Self in the lead, try to communicate that to this protector. Ask what it thinks needs to happen for it to trust you to take the lead with triggering people. If it is skeptical or has concerns about fully trusting you to do this, ask if it can tell you more about that.

10. When it feels right, thank this protector for practicing this way with you and for all it was able to show or express to you in this exercise. Ask it if there is anything else it would like to share with you now or at a later time.

11. Check in with any of the parts that were present as you began this exercise, noting their reactions or concerns, and thank them for remaining in the background as you did this.

12. Say goodbye for now, and spend some time journaling or drawing about this experience if it feels right.

Firefighter Mapping

What You'll Need

- 20 to 40 minutes of uninterrupted time
- A large piece of blank paper, a sketchpad, or journal
- Colored pencils, markers, or a pen

Overview

A powerful way to identify and externalize a "cluster" of the parts in our internal family system is to create a map of them. You may find this useful as you continue to work to unblend from and further deepen your relationships with your firefighters. This can help you visualize the internal relationships they have both with one another and with you, the Self. It can also reveal particular patterns that play out among them over time as well (though you may need to revise the map as you learn more). Allow your firefighters to guide you with the ways in which they want to be depicted on your map. Remember that this representation can take shape in whatever way makes sense for you. It can be more of a diagram with lots of writing, it might be more artistic with colors and images/shapes, or it could be a unique combination of the two.

Instructions

1. Settle into a comfortable place where you can write or draw easily, and take several deep breaths. Turn your attention inward and ask that any of the firefighters you may have already met and have been working with be present with you now. If you don't notice any parts emerging right away, check in with your body to see what parts might be drawing your awareness through bodily sensations.

2. Note how you feel toward these parts. Listen to the concerns of any other parts that may be reacting to them and then ask them to kindly relax if they can; let them know that they can be part of this experience, too, if they'd like.

3. Draw a symbol, sign, design, or shape that can represent you (the Self), placing this somewhere near the center of the page. This could be just a circle or whatever feels right.

4. Now, focus again on the part or parts that are present and check with them to see how and where they'd like to be depicted on the page. What type of symbol, shape, or image would they like to appear as, and where in relation to the Self do they want to be? Do they want to use colors, designs, or words to express who they are on the map? Would they like you to write in their name or role in some way?

5. Write or draw whatever your firefighters express about themselves on your map. Also ask how they would like the relationships between them to be shown there. Are they close to one another, or to you, or far apart? Should there be any indication of particular boundaries or special connections between them?

6. Continue to fill in the map with these parts until it feels complete to you for now, and ask them if there is any story they feel should go with it, or any other parts that they are connected to that should be there as well.

7. Thank these parts for everything they were able to share in this process. Even if only one part participated in this activity, you can continue to add to this map as you come to know more of your parts over time.

8. Now look at your "firefighter map" and reflect on what you notice either on the page or in your journal.

CHAPTER SIX

Challenges and Strategies

As your Self-led IFS journey progresses, you're likely to encounter some challenging terrain from time to time. This chapter will assist you in understanding and working with the most common issues that are likely to emerge along the way. It will also offer some helpful strategies for support in this continued exploration of your inner world.

Polarized Parts

Disagreements and conflicts arise in all families; our internal family is no exception. When disputes occur between two or more of our parts, it's understandably difficult for them to get along. Given the limits of their perspectives and the strength of their convictions, they each think they know the "right" way to protect the system. As this dynamic continues over time, the two "sides" of the polarization often become more extreme, creating an internal power struggle. Each part comes to believe the worst about the other and is determined to *not* allow the opposing side to gain more influence and take over.

Outside of this battle, we can see they're both attempting to prevent exposure of the deeper vulnerability they are each charged with protecting, which is usually the exiles' pain. Unfortunately, they can't see it because they don't trust each other. They then become locked in a cycle of conflict. It's as if these parts are on a sailboat they fear is about to overturn: As one leans way out on one side of the boat to prevent this, the other has to simultaneously lean out equally far in the opposite direction. They believe they must remain in these extreme positions to stay afloat, and they're both right—if either were to unilaterally leave their post and move toward the center of the boat, it would capsize.

Clearly the parts caught in this predicament need the help of a neutral third party whose guidance and authority they can both recognize and trust. So, once we unblend from these parts and any others that are impacted, Self is available to mediate and relate to each with compassion and respect. In his teachings, Dr. Richard C. Schwartz explains that "polarizations need your loving presence," which is truly the key to help each side become less extreme and to really *listen* to each other, which is exactly what they've *not* been able to do on their own. Our presence also allows full awareness and appreciation of the polarization itself, along with the considerable amount of energy involved in maintaining the conflict. In offering this, we encourage these parts to come to understand each other from a more spacious vantage point, emphasizing that neither intends harm and that they actually share a common purpose.

When working with our polarized parts, it's important to be aware that these power struggles can occur between two managers, two firefighters, a protector and an exile, or even among several parts invested in the conflict. They typically arise between our managers and firefighters, however, as those are the parts that most frequently activate each other and quarrel. There may also be another manager in the mix that is working very hard to figure it out but has been unsuccessful.

With all this going on, it's essential to consistently check to determine the degree to which you may be blended with any of the parts involved, as intervening from Self won't be effective if you're favoring one part over the other. Our parts that are stuck in a polarization can only begin to relax and become more open to their sparring partner(s) when they feel seen, heard, and fully validated by the Self. Once they do, they can hopefully begin to function better as a team.

TIP: If you struggle with the unblending process, it can be helpful to ask someone you trust to hold space for you and lend you some of their Self-energy. We all know how helpful it can be to "phone a friend" for support during times of heightened distress. Having someone hold space for you while you work with your parts can be similarly helpful, so long as the person you choose is open to the IFS process and has the ability to keep the focus squarely on your experience. They can assist you just by asking frequently, "Can you tell how you feel toward that part?" Offering this gentle inquiry can encourage more spaciousness inside you and help you find your way back to Self. Just be sure to ask someone who has the ability to follow your lead and the capacity to join you in embodying some degree of Self-energy, too.

Step-by-Step: Working with a Polarization

1. Settle into a comfortable position and take a few deep breaths. Note areas of tension or energy in the body and become aware of what parts are present and may be primarily involved in the conflict.

2. Notice how you feel toward each of these parts and respectfully request that any other reactive parts relax after you've listened to and validated their concerns.

3. Once you are present in Self (feeling curious, open, interested, concerned, etc.) toward each polarized part, ask which would

like to talk with you first, or notice which one seems to need your attention right away. If you sense a part that wants to "figure out" the problem or situation, start with that one, and ask the others to listen respectfully and not interrupt as they wait for their turn.

4. Ask the one that has stepped forward to tell or show you what its role is or what it is trying to do for you in this dispute, what it feels the disagreement is about, and what is making this so difficult from its perspective. Thank this part, and request that it now step to the side and respectfully listen as you check in with other parts.

5. Now, turning toward the other part(s), check to see how you feel toward them, and unblend again from any other reactive parts. Repeat step four with this part(s), and thank them for their openness.

6. Reflect back what each part has expressed to you, validating their positions and difficulties, and invite them to discuss their responses to what the other has shared.

7. Ask if they might be willing to speak directly with the other part, and continue to unblend as necessary. Reassure them that you'll make sure they interact respectfully and without getting extreme, if they are willing.

8. Check in with both to see if they are beginning to understand each other better, and whether they feel there is some common ground between them. Remind them that both are important and that neither can have too much control inside.

9. Discuss with both parts what they see as possibilities for resolving this conflict, making sure that potential solutions come from *them*, not you or another "helping" part. If they do come up with something, check back with each one to make sure that they're both relatively satisfied with this arrangement. Ask what they

might need from you, Self, to help them hold their agreement in place.

10. Express your gratitude to both sides for their willingness to work this out together. Let them know you intend to continue to assist them in whatever way they might need moving forward (e.g., reminding them about their agreement, checking back every day for a while to help them monitor how it's going, etc.).

TIP: "Holding Both Sides" on page 157 and "The Conference Table Technique" on page 161 are designed to assist you further in working with your polarizations.

Parts Stuck in Extreme Roles

Attending to our polarizations involves at least two parts that have taken on extreme positions in the system, but there are also times when we experience this with just one. Such activation can occur with any of our protectors as well as with our exiles for a number of reasons. One cause we've discussed is that an individual part is caught in a difficult polarization. Another could be that the part is protecting an extremely burdened exile, and it might be working even harder at the moment to keep that exile safe or from overwhelming the system with its pain. Often the burdens our exiles must carry are very intense and may hold a lot of shame, which makes it necessary for their protectors to do whatever it takes to keep such burdens hidden.

There is also the possibility that these parts are stuck in the past. This is usually the case for our exiles but can frequently be true of our highly charged protectors as well. Often there are parts of us that were forced into their extreme roles due to circumstances in childhood when the resources we needed were unavailable to us. They then continue to function as if we currently lack the support necessary to meet our needs.

One other important reason a part might become extreme is that something external to the system is activating such a reaction, such as conflict in a relationship or the stress of a demanding job or financial worries, for example. This is a very common occurrence, and we usually know that it's happening once we've been able to cultivate enough internal awareness to begin to track some of the patterns of reactivity that play out with our parts. But, depending on the nature or severity of the triggering event, it can also be quite challenging to deal with on our own.

When faced with any part that is functioning in an extreme way, it is crucial to bring as much Self-energy to it as possible. We all need help doing this from time to time because, when extreme, parts naturally feel the need to blend with us. So, this may be a situation in which engaging the help of a compassionate, nonjudgmental friend or IFS therapist would be particularly helpful so that *you*, the Self, can be present *with* the activated part, rather than *being* that part. Once this occurs, you can truly begin to understand and befriend any part stuck in an extreme position from a place of curiosity and concern. You can actually then turn *toward* even the most extreme of your parts and see the complexity of their dilemmas, validate that they have a good reason for showing up this way, and encourage them to reveal more of their stories.

Step-by-Step: Helping a Part Stuck in an Extreme Role

1. If your system is currently activated, take a few minutes to engage in whichever of the breathing or movement practices from chapter 2 you found helpful.

2. Settle yourself into a comfortable position, breathing deeply from the belly, and with your breath, send some calming energy to any areas of the body that feel constricted, agitated, tense, or even painful.

3. If possible, notice how you feel toward these bodily sensations and whether they are connected to a part that feels "extreme" in its reactivity (which they likely are). If you sense other parts reacting, acknowledge and validate their concerns and ask that they relax or step off to the side if they can.

4. Now, ask yourself again how you feel toward the part that feels extreme, and unblend again until you're feeling more open, curious, neutral, or compassionate. See if you can let the part know how you're feeling toward it once you reach this point.

5. If this part continues to feel highly charged and other parts are still reactive, see if you can "breathe yourself bigger." In other words, try to breathe in more space around these parts to increase a feeling of spaciousness, which can help you to be present with them more easily. (This technique comes from long-time IFS senior trainer and mentor Kay Gardner, LCPC.)

6. Once you can feel more spaciousness, ask any other reactive parts to let you know who they are and what they're concerned about right now. As you listen and validate each one's concerns, respectfully request that they sit back a bit and allow you to be with the primary activated part.

7. If the "extreme" part is continuing to find it difficult to unblend from you, ask it if it can allow there to be just a little bit of separation between you and it so that you can be present *with* it. If it's able to do this, express your appreciation.

8. Now, ask this part to let you know whatever it needs to about what it's going through, what it's trying to do for you by being this extreme, who or what it's protecting, and anything else it would like to share with you.

9. Continue just being present with and listening to this part, and if it feels right, you can ask it the following questions:

   • How old do you think I am right now?
   • Would you like to know how things are/what our life is like now?
   • Is there anything I may not be aware of that is keeping you activated right now, internally or externally?

10. Update the part regarding your age and current life circumstances, while continuing to listen and validate its experience surrounding either being triggered or stuck in its current role.

11. Now, inquire whether there is anything this part needs from you or could use your help with. Discuss together how best to provide it this assistance.

12. Offer your sincere gratitude and compassion to this part for having the courage to unblend enough to be present with you and for helping you better understand its dilemma. Let it know you will continue to be in contact with it and help it in the days ahead.

TIP: For support with being with a part stuck in an extreme role, check out "The Four Drawing Exercise" on page 164 and "The 8 Cs Meditation" on page 167.

Contact with an Exile

Invariably there will be times while on your IFS journey that you either sense or directly encounter one or more of your vulnerable exiled parts. It's only natural that this will occur as we work with our protectors, especially those in extreme roles. Such triggering can usually be traced back to an exile that is hurting and in need of care. So, as we discussed when setting out on this path, we will not delve into the complete process of unburdening that is necessary to fully release our exiles from their pain. Most of us require additional support to do so. Offering guidance to engage with an exile *from Self* is extremely important, though, as our exiles are also valuable members of our internal family and deserve to be welcomed as they arise.

When we notice the deep emotion or troubling distress of an exile, it's essential to keep in mind a couple of foundational principles that are referred to in IFS as "laws of inner physics." They can apply to challenges with any of our parts but have particular relevance in considering the nature of our exiles, especially when they're triggered.

The first law asserts that when we request that a part not overwhelm us with its powerful feelings, it won't. While this is found to be quite universally true, the one caveat is that it only works if we ask this *from Self*, and not from another part. This can be tricky to do when a protective part is really blended with us as we are sensing an exile or when other parts are particularly activated. Such reactivity points to the second guiding principle, which states that Self *can* be with and tolerate the emotional intensity of our exiles, but because our protectors don't trust this is true, they often interfere in our attempts. Protecting us from the exiles' pain is their job after all, so this makes perfect sense. Once we unblend from and validate the concerns of these hardworking protectors and reassure them that we only want to acknowledge the exile, they will usually be more open to letting us do this.

Another helpful point to know is that parts can reduce the intensity of their reactions if they are asked to. It is incredibly important to remind all the parts involved that we can gently request that the exile "turn down" the degree of its intensity, even just a little, to make more room for Self to be with it. Allowing the exile and its protectors to be fully aware that you care and can listen with compassion increases their trust and sense of safety. So when we come upon an exile, just being as present as possible, in Self, is extremely important. This way we can recognize and let it know we won't forget about it, which is quite impactful, and is a gift that we can offer it.

Step-by-Step: Being with an Exile

1. If you are currently experiencing significant emotional activation, take a few minutes to engage in whichever of the breathing or movement practices from chapter 2 you found helpful.

2. Find a comfortable position, either sitting up tall or lying down, and take a few deep breaths.

3. If you're sensing the energy of an exile in your body, such as deep emotional pain like shame, loneliness, or despair, it may be helpful to place one hand on the area where you're noticing it and the other where you might be feeling some Self-energy, such as your heart or your "center" (just above your belly button). See if you can, with your breath or however it feels right to you, extend Self-energy toward the part.

4. As you do this, ask yourself how you feel toward this part, noticing whether there are any protectors present that may be reacting. If there are, validate their concerns, ask for their permission to simply *be with* this exile, and offer them reassurance that you can request that the exile not overwhelm you.

5. Extend your appreciation to these protectors, letting them know that you only want to meet the exile. Discuss any further concerns they have, recognizing that they have very good reasons for these worries and that you won't proceed if they still feel strongly that you shouldn't.

6. If the protectors do grant their permission, notice now where you're experiencing the energy of the exile and how you feel toward it. Unblend from any additional parts that may be reacting at this point, offering the same reassurance to them as in step five.

7. Once you're present, in Self, with the exile, feeling some concern, kindness, curiosity, openness, or compassion toward it, let it know this in whatever way you can, as you continue to offer it calming breaths.

8. If you start to feel overwhelmed by the exile's emotions, ask if it can "turn down the volume" of those feelings just a little bit so that you can stay present with it, and thank it for doing this if it is able to.

9. See if you can surround this part with your compassion, letting it know that there is nothing to do but to just *be* together. Notice how it responds to you. You can reinforce this compassion with loving physical gestures, like holding your hand on your heart or belly (or wherever you feel the exile's energy), or gently hugging yourself.

10. While continuing to extend your love and appreciation to this part, see if you can open your heart to it even more, and gently ask if there is anything it would like to share with you or anything that it needs right now. Listen closely and offer your support. Let it know that it's OK if it doesn't say much and that it could also show you whatever it can to feel seen and acknowledged by you.

11. Continue sending it love and gratitude for being with you now and for whatever it's been able to share. Express to this part how much you value it and that you'll find someone to assist you in helping it more. Let it know you won't forget about it and will check in with it if it would like you to do that.

12. Say goodbye to this exile and extend additional appreciation to the other parts that graciously stepped back so that you could be with it.

TIP: "The 8 Cs Meditation" on page 167 is a guided meditation that can be used to help you continue to be present with an exile. "The Four Drawing Exercise" on page 164 can also be helpful for understanding more about your exiles, as it is useful with any of our parts.

Holding Both Sides

What You'll Need

- 20 to 40 minutes of uninterrupted time
- Two or three throw pillows (if desired)
- Your journal, sketchpad, blank paper, or digital notebook
- A pen, pencil, markers, or colored pencils (as desired)

Overview

This exercise presents a strategy to help external-ize two parts that are polarized with each other. This often happens when we are struggling to make an important decision or are feeling pulled in differ-ent directions. It's a tool that will enable you to use physical space to make it easier to hold conversa-tions with each part involved and can be extremely beneficial to further unblend from these parts so that Self can be fully present as a compassionate mediator.

Instructions

1. Sit, lie down, or stand in a relaxed position. Take a few slow, deep breaths and allow yourself to notice bodily sensations, images, or words that feel connected to your polarized parts. Notice where in your body you're feeling these parts. Which part emerges first or which is drawing your attention more?

2. Check to see if there is another part present that seems to be trying to mediate or figure out the problem. If you do find a "mediator" manager, thank it for working so hard in this situation. Ask about and validate its concerns, and reassure it that it can relax right now (and can watch) while you work with the polar-ized parts.

3. Turn back toward the polarized parts and check to see how you feel toward each of them. If there are other parts reacting to each

one, acknowledge and validate their concerns and respectfully ask that they step back.

4. Once you are present with the two polarized parts from a place of concern, curiosity, openheartedness, etc., let them know this, adding that your intention is not to change or fix anything, but to listen to and support them both.

5. Now, turn your palms up in your lap or at your sides, and invite these parts to each bring their energy into one of your hands so that you can "hold" them each in this way. (If this doesn't feel quite right to you or these parts, ask that they sit on pillows on either side of you or in chairs and arrange things accordingly.)

6. Notice what it's like to hold them both and ask what it feels like to them. Check again to see how you feel toward them, asking any reactive parts to again step back, and let the polarized parts know that you will listen to them both.

7. Ask the parts which one would like to speak with you first or notice which seems to need your attention first, and then do the following:

   a) Direct your awareness to the hand or "side" of the part chosen to start. Ask it what concerns it has about you listening to the other part. Validate these concerns, and ask what it worries will happen if it relaxes in its stance.

   b) Ask what this part's intention is for you in the midst of this struggle, and whether or not it's protecting another part right now. Now, ask this part to let you know what it needs to feel safe as you talk with the other part, and if there is anything else it needs you to know.

   c) Thank this part and ask it to listen respectfully while you interact with the other part.

8. When you feel ready, bring your attention to the other part. Thank it for waiting as you spoke with the first part, and then do the following:

   a) Ask this part what it was like for it to listen as you talked with the first part, and whether or not anything came up for it as it did.

   b) Listen to everything this part needs to tell you, also asking it about its intention for you in the dispute with the first part, whether it is protecting another part, and what it's worried will happen if it talks directly with the other part.

   c) If it feels right, ask whether these parts are protecting the same exile and whether they share other common concerns.

   d) Ask this part how it is feeling now toward the first part and whether it still feels so opposed to it, along with anything else it wants to share with you regarding what it needs to feel safe while being with the other part.

   e) Thank this part, validate its concerns, and offer reassurance that you will work to help them both feel safe, respected, and heard in this interaction.

9. Now bring your attention to both hands (or sides), and check to see how you feel toward both of these parts now. If you notice any other parts reacting, ask about and validate their concerns and request that they step back and relax so that you can continue the conversation with the polarized parts.

10. Ask each polarized part if it is aware of the other and what it thinks or feels about what the other shared in terms of what each is trying to do for you and the part(s) it may be protecting. Listen closely as each part speaks.

11. Ask each part about what it heard from the other in terms of an intention for the current struggle and any ideas for some sort of resolution. Ask them to reflect on what it's like for them to be interacting this way and to have you present with them as they do.

12. See if there is anything more you want to let them know about what you noticed may be "common ground" or anything they need to have happen from what they shared to help the conflict. Ask them each to reflect on what might work as a way to represent the needs and concerns that both have in terms of moving into a more collaborative relationship.

13. Reassure them that you can all continue to discuss and monitor their progress in this effort and that taking their time with this makes sense. Let them know they can each express any concerns about this to you now or as they arise and that you want to continue to support them.

14. When you and they feel ready, invite these parts to move their energy back inside, expressing your gratitude for trusting you to be present with them and for the courage it took for them to interact with each other. Ask if there is anything else either part would like to express to you or to the other part.

15. Extend your appreciation to any other parts that stepped back throughout this process. Let them know that you are open to discussing their reactions and concerns as well. Say goodbye for now to the parts you worked with and any that reacted in the process. Note or draw about what you learned from them in your journal.

The Conference Table Technique

What You'll Need

- 20 to 60 minutes of uninterrupted time
- A sketchpad, large piece of blank paper, and your journal
- A pen, markers, and colored pencils as desired

Overview

This technique allows you to externalize an entire group of your parts in a way that each of them can be heard and recognized for their unique perspectives and contributions to the internal family system. It is an incredibly helpful way to "hold meetings" of multiple parts that may have concerns about or are polarized around a particular issue. This technique was introduced to the IFS community by Michi Rose, PhD, an early collaborator in the development of the IFS model. She adapted it from an original concept she learned from Dr. AlixSandra Parness.

Instructions

1. Settle into a comfortable space where you can write or draw easily, and take a few slow, deep breaths. Allow your awareness to turn inward, noticing any particular physical sensations, thoughts, or images that may be present.

2. Bring to mind an issue you'd like to explore or that you know a number of your parts have concerns about. Or if you are already aware of a group of parts that are polarized or in conflict about something, ask them to be present with you now.

3. As these parts step forward, check to see how you feel toward each one. If other parts are reacting as you do this, acknowledge and validate their concerns, and let them know that they can also be present in this experience.

4. Ask each reactive part to step aside briefly so that you can be present with each part that needs to join the discussion first. Continue unblending from each part that steps forward until you have the sense that all parts with concerns are present.

5. Ask the parts that have gathered to sit down together in a circle. This can be around a large conference table, a kitchen table, a campfire, etc. You and they can decide whichever option feels best. Find a way to represent this on paper; it could just be a big circle or more detailed.

6. Ask the parts how they would like to be represented around the circle, who they want to sit next to, etc., and write or draw them as it feels right. Be sure to include any of the parts that stepped back previously, and check to see if any other parts would also like to be present.

7. Situate yourself wherever it feels right in the circle, letting all the parts gathered know that you would like to hear from each of them in turn, and ask if it would be helpful to write out the concerning issue at the top of the page (and do that if they would like you to).

8. Invite all the parts gathered to take turns speaking about their concerns. Ask each one to share their perspective on the issue being discussed along with their concerns about any of the other parts.

9. Remind the group that remaining as open and respectful as possible in this discussion is important and that what each part shares is valuable. Let each part know that it can have many turns if necessary.

10. Notice who needs to speak first and who may be talking a lot. Continue to let them all know that you'd like to hear from everyone. Let the group know that you are most interested in hearing

their truth, that this may have many layers to it, and that it might change a bit as the discussion continues.

11. Check to see that the group is able to hear what each part shares, and record the key points of the discussion if it feels right. Notice whether there are any new, previously undiscovered ideas available to address the issue being discussed. If so, share your realizations with the group.

12. Express your appreciation to the group for their courage and creativity. Thank them for coming together in this way, for sharing all they've been able to share, and for working together on your behalf. Inquire about any additional concerns that have not yet been shared.

13. Reassure the group that you will take everything discussed into account as you continue to work with the issue. Remind these parts that you will be the one to make whatever decisions are necessary around this issue and how much you value their input.

14. Say goodbye for now, letting them know that you are available to them whenever the need arises.

15. Spend some time journaling or drawing about what you've learned.

The Four Drawing Exercise

What You'll Need

- 20 to 60 minutes of uninterrupted time
- Four pieces of blank paper or four blank pages in your journal
- Markers, colored pencils or pens, or crayons

Overview

This is a creative (and often very powerful) technique for helping any part that may be struggling with a particular issue or that you sense is "blocked" in some way. It helps you embody that part's struggle as well as what the potential transformation of this part might look like. Based on an original concept by James Kowal, PhD, it was developed and expanded by longtime IFS senior trainer Michi Rose, PhD. It is essential to follow the directions for numbering the pages closely, even though this may seem a bit unusual. It will all make sense in the end!

Instructions

1. Find a comfortable position that will allow you to write and draw easily in a space where you can move your body if you choose, and take a few deep breaths.

2. Notice or invite in the part you'd like to spend time with, and see how you feel toward it. Ask any reactive parts about their concerns and validate these, and request that they step back so that you can work with this part, thanking them as they do.

3. See what you notice about this part. What is its role inside? Is there anything it wants you to know about itself? Represent this part in whatever way feels right to you, using lines, colors, and words on the first piece of paper, and label this "page 1."

4. Allow yourself to imagine what transformation of this part would be like. How might this part manifest if unburdened or if it were able to let go of its job or role? Represent the transformation on the next piece of paper with colors, lines, shapes, and words. Label this "page 4."

5. Stand up and embody the target part as you have represented it on page 1. See if you can physically sense the contractions, burdens, and internal struggle of this part. If it doesn't feel right to you to embody this part, just notice how it feels inside as you tune into it more.

6. Now move over to the feeling of transformation on page 4, and notice the opening and expansion of this in your body.

7. If it feels right, move back and forth from the struggle or burden to the release (between pages 1 and 4). Is there some internal wisdom or a "solution" that is emerging as you do this? What needs to happen *inside* for the transformation to happen?

8. Using a fresh piece of paper, draw the wisdom or solution using words, lines, shapes, and colors, and label this "page 3."

9. Place the three drawings out in front of you. Allow yourself to fully take in the dilemma of your target part and what needs to happen for it to move toward transformation. Without pausing too long, ask yourself, what is blocking this process *inside*? Represent this block on another piece of paper with colors, shapes, and words, and label this one "page 2."

10. Carefully review each page, as follows:

    - On page 4, notice the inner strengths and potential resources available within the target part when released or unburdened.
    - On page 2, see and feel what is blocking Self-energy. (These are often referred to as "trailheads" in IFS.)

- On page 3, consider the internal wisdom that is present for the part's dilemma.

11. Take a moment as you reflect on this experience to write anything else you may be noticing or any insights you have gained.

12. Thank your "stuck" part for having the courage to participate in this experience with you. Tell it whatever you'd like for it to know about how you may be feeling toward it now. Reassure it that you will continue to work with it however it would like you to.

The 8 Cs Meditation

What You'll Need

- 20 to 30 minutes of uninterrupted time
- A recording device (if desired)
- Your journal, sketchpad, or digital notebook
- Colored pencils, markers, or a pen

Overview

This lovely meditation was written by IFS lead trainer Gretchen King, LMFT. It is a centering practice that you can return to again and again as you continue on your IFS path. It can be helpful to use while being present with an exile or any other part that could benefit from just being with you and all the qualities of Self-energy. You may wish to record yourself reading the instructions so that you can stay in the experience internally as you listen to it. You may also want to pause as you notice each quality of Self and jot down anything you're aware of.

Instructions

1. Bring yourself into a comfortable seated position with your shoulders back and a nice, long spine without being tense or rigid. Close your eyes or lower your gaze.

2. Feel the weight of your body on the chair. Feel the floor. Feel how you're supported by the energy of the earth.

3. If you notice your mind wandering or that a particular part is present, see if you can welcome those that wandered in or that one part to be here in this moment with you.

4. As you feel into your whole presence right now, what do you notice? What qualities of Self are with you now as your parts settle and there is a little more stillness?

5. Perhaps a sense of *calm* is there for you. How does calm *feel* in your body? What do you notice?

6. Maybe you feel *connected*—connected within yourself or to others, or connected to something greater. Just notice how *connection* feels and what that brings to you.

7. Is there an experience of *clarity*? Of seeing clearly and knowing easily? Invite that sense of clarity to fill you if it's comfortable. What is that like?

8. Do you feel more *courage* coming forth? How does that show itself to you? Or a *creativity* that begins to flow . . . how can you tune into that?

9. Maybe you don't notice any of those, but there is a spark of *curiosity*. Can you gently breathe into that, and does that spark ignite? What is it like when your body is filled with curiosity?

10. There may be a sense of *confidence* that grows—do you feel bigger or more solid in your body?

11. Are you aware of *compassion*? Is that centered in your heart? Does it open even a little more as you focus there? Allow yourself to just be with that for a moment.

12. Notice which of the 8 Cs was more prominent for you today, and just take a moment to welcome that experience more fully.

13. Maybe there is a different way you feel in alignment with yourself right now. If you didn't experience any of the 8 Cs today, see if you can just acknowledge your experience as valid and know that Self is in and around you, whether or not you feel it.

14. If you are feeling some sense of Self, invite it to extend out to those you live with and others you love, to your community, to our Earth and all who call it home. Envision bringing this sense of Self with you into the rest of your day.

15. When you're ready, open your eyes or lift your gaze, and write or draw about whatever you experienced, as well as what this was like for the part or parts that accompanied you.

My Internal Family

What You'll Need

- 30 to 60 minutes (or more) of un-interrupted time
- A large piece of blank paper, a sketchpad, and your journal
- Colored pencils, markers, or a pen

Overview

This is an opportunity to reflect on your IFS journey so far by bringing together all the parts you discovered along the way in a mapping of your entire internal family system as you see it right now. This is a powerful method for continuing to identify and unblend from your parts as you externalize them this way. The intention of this exercise is to generate more clarity regarding your system as a whole and to allow you to better visualize the relationships between your parts and how they affect one another. You can create your internal family map in whatever way feels right to you. This is your unique representation of what you have learned about your internal family system so far. While it may change over time, it can be a source of validation and recognition for your parts as you continue your healing work together.

Instructions

1. Set yourself up in a comfortable space where you can write or draw easily, and take a few deep breaths.

2. Gather and reflect on the parts maps you created, including the IFS mandala (page 90), your manager map (page 117), and your firefighter map (page 143), as well as your depictions of polarized parts and possibly an exile or a part stuck in an extreme role.

3. As you look over your work, check to see how you feel toward the parts that are present on these maps. If there are any other parts reacting, ask them about and validate any concerns they may have, and let them know they can be represented in the map you will create now.

4. Notice what may have shifted or changed since you completed your earlier maps and what stands out to you in terms of how these parts are in relationship to each other. Are there particular alliances or conflictual relationships that emerge? Are protectors connected to vulnerable parts in a particular way?

5. Start your new map by drawing a symbol or shape that represents you, the Self, and place this somewhere near the center of the page (this can be just a circle or whatever feels right). If you prefer to use the IFS mandala for this exercise, draw a large, blank version of that on your page (see page 91 for help). Alternatively, you could draw another structure to reflect how you view your consciousness (see "Understanding Your Psyche" on page 35 for ideas from the metaphors discussed there).

6. Take a moment to check inside for any guidance from your parts about whether they would like to be shown in the same way you previously drew or wrote about them or if they'd like something different now. Begin to fill in your map with the parts you now know or have some awareness of, again, in whatever way they may want to be represented.

7. Where in relation to you does it feel right for these parts to be—quite close or far away? Are they connected to you in a particular way? Using lines, shapes, colors, or words, show how close your parts are to one another. Are there boundaries or special connections between them that need to be shown in some way?

8. Continue to capture all you can about your parts and their relationships among themselves and to you, adding words and any narrative that feels important as you do.

9. Check in with the parts that are represented on your map to see if this feels right to them. Ask them if they are aware of any other parts that also need to be shown. If they do know of other parts, see if those parts can let you know how they would like to be depicted. Do that until the map feels complete to you and to all the parts involved.

10. Once this feels complete, hold your map out in front of you, at a bit of a distance, so that you can get a wider perspective on the whole thing. What relationship patterns do you notice now? How do you feel toward these parts as you see them in this way? Is there a way you'd like to include this on your map?

11. Thank all your parts for being present with you in this way and for sharing all that they have, both in this exercise and in all your work with them so far. Check with these parts to see if there is anything more they'd like to share with you right now. Reassure them that you will continue to be in contact with them as your healing path unfolds.

12. As you reflect on your more comprehensive map and your Self-led IFS journey to this point, note in your journal or on your map any particular insights or next steps that feel important as you conclude this exercise for now.

Conclusion

It has been my honor and privilege to accompany you to this point on your IFS journey. In many ways, it is one of coming home to that wise, compassionate, and loving place within that is always available to us—our true Self. It is also a path of understanding ourselves in all our unique complexity, even and especially when we stumble along the way.

Author, professor, and speaker Brené Brown shares this perspective when she writes in *Atlas of the Heart*, "So often, when we feel lost, adrift in our lives, our first instinct is to look out into the distance to find the nearest shore. But that shore, that solid ground is within us. The anchor we are searching for is connection and it is internal."

My hope for you is that you continue to cultivate your awareness and connection to that solid ground within you, and I congratulate you for all that you have accomplished so far on this adventure of Self-discovery. I wish you well in all your travels!

Glossary

BLENDING: When the feelings and beliefs of one part merge with or "take over" another part or the Self.

BURDENS: Extreme beliefs or feeling states carried by parts, which are absorbed from frightening or shaming experiences, interactions, or events and remain within those parts.

EXILES: Vulnerable, usually young parts that are sequestered out of consciousness, either for their own protection or to protect the rest of the system from being overwhelmed by their extreme emotions or beliefs.

FIREFIGHTERS: Parts who react quickly, aiming either to calm the exiled part or to distract from exiled feelings and beliefs that have been evoked.

MANAGERS: Parts who run the system in ways that aim to minimize the activation (distress) of its exiled parts.

MULTIPLICITY PARADIGM: A conceptual view of the human mind as plural or naturally subdivided into a multitude of "parts."

PARTS: The term used in the Internal Family Systems model for a person's subpersonalities. Parts are considered to be internal beings of different ages, talents, and temperaments, and can appear in many different forms (people, animals, objects, etc.).

POLARIZATION: A state in which two members (or two groups) in the same system take opposing views and are in conflict or compete for influence in that system. They each grow increasingly extreme out of fear that the other side will take over and can thereby obscure the Self.

SELF: The "core" or seat of consciousness of a person, which is characterized by qualities such as perspective, presence, patience, playfulness, persistence, curiosity, creativity, calm, clarity, caring, connectedness, confidence, and compassion. The Self is the only inner entity that is fully equipped to lead the internal family.

SELF-ENERGY: The perspectives and feelings the Self brings into the relationship with the parts that compose the internal family system.

SELF-LED: Describes individuals who have access to their Self, and therefore have the capacity to hear, understand, and be present with their parts, acknowledging and appreciating the importance of their roles in the internal family system and with other people.

UNBLENDED: The state of being in which no part (e.g., feeling, thought, sensation, belief) takes over, merges, or blends with the Self, often experienced as internal spaciousness and clear cognition.

UNBURDENING: The process in which an exiled part lets go of the painful emotions and beliefs it has been carrying. This often involves a ceremonial release internally. After unburdening, the part invites qualities of its own choosing to come into itself and fill the space within it made by releasing the burden.

Resources

Books

Altogether You: Experiencing Personal and Spiritual Transformation with Internal Family Systems Therapy by Jenna Riemersma (Pivotal Press, 2020)

Bring Yourself to Love: How Couples Can Turn Disconnection into Intimacy by Mona Barbera (Dos Monos Press, 2008)

Compassionate Mediation for Relationships at a Crossroad: How to Add Passion to Your Marriage or Compassion to Your Divorce by Linda Kroll (Compassionate Communication, 2016)

Daily Parts Meditation Practice: A Journey of Embodied Integration for Clients and Therapists (2nd ed.) by Michelle Glass (The Listen3r, 2016)

Internal Family Systems Therapy for Addictions: Trauma-Informed, Compassion-Based Interventions for Substance Use, Eating, Gambling and More by Cece Sykes, Martha Sweezy, and Richard C. Schwartz (PESI Publishing, 2023)

The Internal Family Systems Workbook: A Guide to Discover Your Self and Heal Your Parts by Richard C. Schwartz (Sounds True, 2024)

Many Minds, One Self: Evidence for a Radical Shift in Paradigm by Richard C. Schwartz and Robert R. Falconer (Trailheads Publications, 2017)

No Bad Parts: Healing Trauma and Restoring Wholeness with the Internal Family Systems Model by Richard C. Schwartz (Sounds True, 2021)

The Parts Inside of Me by Shelly Johnson (Archway Publishing, 2020)

Parts Work: An Illustrated Guide to Your Inner Life (Book 1 of 2: Parts Work) by Tom Holmes (Winged Heart Press, 2007)

Parts Work: A Path of the Heart: Healing Journeys Integrating IFS and Spirituality (Book 2 of 2: Parts Work) by Tom Holmes (Winged Heart Press, 2022)

Self-Compassion Day by Day: Daily Reflections with Internal Family Systems by Karen A. Locke (Independently published, 2019)

Self-Led: Living a Connected Life With Yourself and With Others: An Application of Internal Family Systems by Seth Kopald (Exploration Services, 2023)

Somatic Internal Family Systems Therapy: Awareness, Breath, Resonance, Movement, and Touch in Practice by Susan McConnell (North Atlantic Books, 2020)

The Somatic Internal Family Systems Therapy Workbook: A Therapist's Guide to the 5 Practices of Somatic IFS for Transforming Trauma in Clients by Susan McConnell (North Atlantic Books, 2025)

The Spirit-Led Life: A Christian Encounter with Internal Family Systems: Mary Steege Interviews with Richard C. Schwartz by Mary Steege (Independently published, 2010)

You Are the One You've Been Waiting For: Applying Internal Family Systems to Intimate Relationships by Richard C. Schwartz (Sounds True, 2023)

Audio Recordings

Coming Home: Guided Meditations for Inner Connection, Intimacy from the Inside Out, Volumes 1 and 2 by Toni Herbine-Blank (ToniHerbineBlank.com)

Websites

The Foundation for Self Leadership
FoundationIFS.org

The Internal Family Systems Counselling Association (Derek Scott, founder)
IFSCA.ca

The Internal Family Systems Institute
IFS-Institute.com

The Integral Guide to Well-Being by Levi
IntegralGuide.com

Jenna Riemersma
JennaRiemersma.com

Podcasts and Video Series

IFS Counselling Association—Derek IFSCA—Video Series (YouTube)
@IFSCA

IFS Therapy with Alessio—Video Series (YouTube)
@ifstherapywithalessio494

Life Architect—IFS Therapy & More, Michael Pasterski—Video Series (YouTube)

@lifearchitectcom

Self Therapy and Internal Family Systems (IFS), Conor McMillen—Video Series (YouTube)

@selftherapyIFS

The One Inside: An Internal Family Systems Podcast with Tammy Sollenberger

TheOneInside.libsyn.com

Tori Olds, PhD—Video Series (YouTube)

toriolds.com/transformation-series

"Dr. Richard Schwartz: A Systems Approach to Healing the Self," episode #761 of *The Rich Roll Podcast*

richroll.com/podcast/richard-schwartz-761

"No Bad Parts w/ Richard Schwartz," from *The Psychology Podcast with Scott Barry Kaufman*

scottbarrykaufman.com/podcast/no-bad-parts-w-richard-schwartz

Apps

IFS Guide
IFSGuide.com

Insight Timer: IFS Meditations
InsightTimer.com

Sentur: Inspired by the IFS model
Sentur.app

References

Baxter, Sukie. "Whole Body Revolution." Accessed June 3, 2024. whole-bodyrevolution.com.

Brantbjerg, Merete Holm. "Hyporesponse: The Hidden Challenge in Coping with Stress." *International Body Psychotherapy Journal* 11, no. 2 (2012): 95–118. ibpj.org/issues/articles/Holm%20Brantbjerg%20-%20Hyporesponse.pdf.

Brown, Brené. *Atlas of the Heart: Mapping Meaningful Connection and the Language of Human Experience.* New York: Random House, 2021.

Culver, Ruth. "Resources: The Survive/Thrive Spiral." Calm Heart. Accessed June 4, 2024. calmheart.co.uk/resources.

Dana, Deb. *The Polyvagal Theory in Therapy: Engaging the Rhythm of Regulation.* New York: W. W. Norton, 2018.

Dana, Deborah. "A Beginner's Guide to Polyvagal Theory." PTSD–ADHD: Resource Center for PTSD and ADHD. Accessed June 6, 2024. ptsd-adhd.com/wp-content/uploads/2017/11/Beginners-Guide-Polyvagal.pdf.

Dieffenbach, Linda. "10 Ways to Ground Your Energy." *Wellness in Harmony* (blog). January 12, 2021. wellnessinharmony.com/10-ways-to-ground-your-energy.

Emerson, Ralph Waldo. *Self-Reliance.* New York: Peter Pauper Press, 1967.

Epstein, Mark, MD. *The Trauma of Everyday Life.* New York: Penguin Books, 2013.

Fogel, Alan. *Body Sense: The Science and Practice of Embodied Self-Awareness* (Norton Series on Interpersonal Neurobiology). New York: W. W. Norton, 2013.

Forbes, Bo. *Bo's Guide: How to Survive + Thrive in 2022*. E-book. Accessed June 7, 2024. deft-mover-4082.ck.page/039d13c7cb.

Gilbert, Elizabeth. *Big Magic: Creative Living Beyond Fear*. New York: Riverhead Books, 2015.

Herbine-Blank, Toni, and Martha Sweezy. *Internal Family Systems Couple Therapy Skills Manual: Healing Relationships with Intimacy from the Inside Out*. Eau Claire, WI: PESI Publishing, 2021.

Holmes, Tom, PhD. *Parts Work: An Illustrated Guide to Your Inner Life*. Kalamazoo, MI: Winged Heart Press, 2007.

Khow, Anthony. "Understanding the Window of Tolerance and How It Affects You." *Mind My Peelings* (blog), April 19, 2019. mindmypeelings.com/blog/window-of-tolerance.

Lebentz, Lou. "Lou with Prof. Stephen Porges." *Trauma Thrivers*, accessed June 7, 2024. Podcast, video, 1:08:12. traumathrivers.com/podcasts-interviews.

Levine, Peter A., PhD. *In an Unspoken Voice: How the Body Releases Trauma and Restores Goodness*. Berkeley: North Atlantic Books, 2010.

Lieberman, Lila. "The Neuroscience of Compassion." *UPLIFT* (blog). uplift.love/the-neuroscience-of-compassion.

McConnell, Susan. *Somatic Internal Family Systems Therapy: Awareness, Breath, Resonance, Movement, and Touch in Practice*. Berkeley: North Atlantic Books, 2020.

Merton, Thomas. *Conjectures of a Guilty Bystander*. New York: Doubleday Religion, 1966.

Miller, Keith. *The Soul of Life* podcast. "Michael Elkin: Befriending Addiction and Suicide with IFS." YouTube video, 4:30. August 26, 2021. youtube.com/watch?v=a9qCeUyJ0HE.

Nakazawa, Donna Jackson. *The Last Best Cure: My Quest to Awaken the Healing Parts of My Brain and Get Back My Body, My Joy, and My Life*. New York: Hudson Street Press/Penguin Group, 2013.

Nepo, Mark. *Seven Thousand Ways to Listen: Staying Close to What Is Sacred*. New York: Atria Books, 2012.

Porges, Stephen W. *Polyvagal Safety: Attachment, Communication, Self-Regulation*. New York: W. W. Norton, 2021.

Rosenberg, Stanley. *Accessing the Healing Power of the Vagus Nerve: Self-Help Exercises for Anxiety, Depression, Trauma, and Autism*. Berkeley: North Atlantic Books, 2017.

Ruden, Ronald A. *When the Past Is Always Present: Emotional Traumatization, Causes, and Cures*. New York: Routledge, 2011.

Schwartz, Richard C. *Internal Family Systems Therapy*. 1st ed. New York: Guilford Press, 1995.

Schwartz, Richard C., and Martha Sweezy. *Internal Family Systems Therapy*. 2nd ed. New York: Guilford Press, 2020.

Schwartz, Richard C., and Robert R. Falconer. *Many Minds, One Self: Evidence for a Radical Shift in Paradigm*. Chicago: Trailheads Publications, 2017.

Schwartz, Richard C. *No Bad Parts: Healing Trauma and Restoring Wholeness with the Internal Family Systems Model*. Boulder, CO: Sounds True, 2021.

———. *You Are the One You've Been Waiting For: Applying Internal Family Systems to Intimate Relationships*. Boulder, CO: Sounds True, 2023.

———. "The Larger Self: Discovering the Core Within Our Multiplicity." *Psychotherapy Networker*, May/June 2004. psychotherapynetworker. org/article/larger-self.

Scott, Elizabeth. "Three Reasons Why People Handle Stress Differently." *Verywell Mind* (blog), updated August 10, 2023. verywellmind.com/ why-do-stressors-affect-people-differently-3145061.

Shepherd, Philip. *Radical Wholeness: The Embodied Present and the Ordinary Grace of Being*. Berkeley: North Atlantic Books, 2017.

Siegel, Daniel J. *The Developing Mind: How Relationships and the Brain Interact to Shape Who We Are*. 3rd ed. New York: Guilford Press, 2020.

Sounds True. "All Parts Welcome—Richard Schwartz, PhD + Elizabeth Gilbert: Creativity & Internal Family Systems." YouTube video, 16:03. Streamed live on May 22, 2023. youtube.com/watch?v=VBYrJOK4Dtk.

Springsteen, Bruce. *Born to Run*. New York: Simon & Schuster, 2016.

Sweezy, Martha. *Internal Family Systems Therapy for Shame and Guilt*. New York: Guilford Press, 2023.

Sykes, Cece, Martha Sweezy, and Richard C. Schwartz. *Internal Family Systems Therapy for Addictions: Trauma-Informed, Compassion-Based Interventions for Substance Use, Eating, Gambling and More*. Eau Claire, WI: PESI Publishing, 2023.

Weintraub, Amy. *Yoga for Your Mood Deck: 52 Ways to Shift Depression and Anxiety*. Boulder, CO: Sounds True, 2021.

Acknowledgments

The experience of writing this book has deepened my appreciation for the immense generosity and support of so many within the vibrant IFS community that I have been privileged to be a part of for the past 25 years. None of this would be possible, of course, without the creativity, determination, courage, and persistence of Richard C. Schwartz for bringing this model into being. I am so thankful to him and to Susan McConnell, Beth O'Neil, Michi Rose, Paul Ginter, Kay Gardner, Cece Sykes, Toni Herbine-Blank, Gretchen King, Martha Sweezy, and countless others who have trained and mentored me and have collaborated with me in training experiences throughout my own IFS journey. Special thanks to Janice Milhem for my author photograph.

I am also enormously grateful to Jan Mullen, Tom Holmes, Michi Rose, Gretchen King, and Cece Sykes for their sharing of original source materials for use in this book (and additionally to Cece for writing the foreword), along with Anne Redmond, Shelly Johnson, Beth Mullen-Houser, Gina Abbeduto, Cindy Gault, Dr. Charles Silberstein, Beth Jerva, Vera Dyke, and especially Jan Mullen for their support, insights, and reference suggestions and materials. Many thanks, as well, to the members of my IFS consultation groups, my past and present clients, and our IFS Great Lakes Retreat circle for the incredible support they've provided throughout this process and for all the learning and wisdom they have shared with me over the years.

My Zeitgeist team at Penguin Random House has been a joy to work with. I am indebted to Clara Song Lee for her outstanding editing expertise as well as her enthusiasm, patience, and encouragement, and to Tahra Seplowin and Carol Rosenberg and Ariel Keith for their support and guidance.

I could not have undertaken this challenge without the unwavering support of my dear friends and family. They include Patricia Fuhst-Wylie, Tracy Gogan, Loulie Meynard, Patty and John Zeichman, Sue Lawrence, Dr. Yun Luke Lu, Carey Ryan, Kelly Kirles, Sara AlRawi, Tim Smalley, Sara Dansky, Melissa Walcott, Lisa Warner, Craig Allen, Ian and Caroline Rosoff, Audrey Gloeckner, and our devoted furry ones, Winnie and Phoebe.

Finally, my gratitude for my husband, Stephen Rosoff, knows no bounds. His presence as a solid anchor of Self-energy amidst the sometimes-choppy waters of this endeavor, embodying the qualities of creativity, care, compassion, and belief in me, has made this project possible. His expert editing abilities, good humor, and openheartedness no matter the challenge throughout this process have been incredible gifts to me—he is truly my moon and stars.

Index

About the Author

Tanis Jo Allen, LMSW, ACSW, is a certified IFS psychotherapist in private practice in Ann Arbor, Michigan. She has been practicing, training in, and teaching the IFS model for more than 25 years, having presented many workshops and trainings in the Midwest and Canada, and as a guest lecturer at the University of Michigan. She earned both her master of social work and her bachelor of arts in psychology from the University of Michigan. Her professional experience includes clinical social work in education, both mental and physical healthcare settings, and hospice care. Her clinical specializations include work with anxiety and depression, all forms of eating disorders, grief, loss and trauma issues, adjustment to physical illness, and relationship concerns. An IFS clinical consultant, she also provides supervision and mentorship to psychotherapists learning the model, and established and directs the IFS Great Lakes Retreat, which is held annually in Northern Michigan.

Hi there,

We hope *The Self-Led Internal Family Systems Workbook* helped you. If you have any questions or concerns about your book, or have received a damaged copy, please contact customerservice@penguinrandomhouse.com. We're here and happy to help.

Also, please consider writing a review on your favorite retailer's website to let others know what you thought of the book.

Sincerely,

The Zeitgeist Team